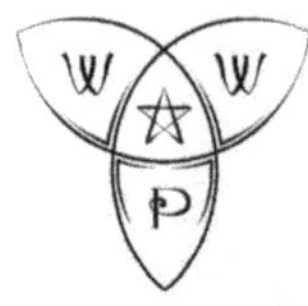

First Edition, 2021

Tonya A. Brown
3436 Magazine St
#460
New Orleans, LA 70115
www.witchwaypublishing.com

Copyright © 2021 by Tonya A. Brown

Editor: Tonya A. Brown
Internal Design: Amanda Smith
Writers: Tonya A. Brown, Amanda Wilson, Kiki Dombrowski

All rights reserved. This book or any portion thereof may not be reproduced or used in any manner whatsoever without the express written permission of the publisher except for the use of brief quotations in a book review.

Printed in the United States of America

ISBN 978-1087915715

Please note that signs and moon phases can depend on your location, if this is a vital part of your practice, always check multiple references.

IF LOST, PLEASE RETURN TO:

DESIGN A SIGIL

A sigil, in short, is a magical symbol. Sigils are designed based on their intended goal. In this case, you will create a sigil specific to this planner. What it will do to or for the planner is up to you – typically sigils are used to protect or empower an object, so you could, for example, design a sigil to protect the planner from theft, loss, or damage.

Another option is to create a sigil that will enchant the planner, so it becomes a magical device that, for instance, enhances your productivity or boosts creativity. There's no wrong way to do this – it's your planner, and you should create a sigil that will serve you best. I have provided the steps for two different methods of sigil design to help you get started on your design.

Chaos Magic Method

Step 1. Compose a clear and concise statement of the intent of the sigil.

Step 2. Remove all the vowels and duplicate letters of the sentence.

Step 3. Combine the remaining letters to create the symbol.

Zakroff Method

I refer to this method as the Zakroff Method because it was created by Laura Tempest Zakroff. Compared to the Chaos magic method, Zakroff's method is designed to be more intuitive and fluid, and, according to Zakroff's Sigil Witchery, it's "accessible to people with a wide variety of abilities and experiences."

Step 1. Identify your goal- what do you want the sigil to do?

Step 2. Brainstorm a list of what you'll need to achieve the goal. For example, if you want the sigil to protect your planner from becoming lost or damaged in any way, you'll come up with symbols to represent protection, the planner, and remaining whole and unharmed.

Step 3. Design the sigil. Find fun ways to put your favorite doodles together in a way that appeals to you aesthetically and magically.

Step 4. Apply the sigil – aka, draw the sigil on the Planner Sigil page. There is no need to charge the final design because the thought and energy put into the creation is more than sufficient to empower the final design.

INTENTION:

Record a Card Pull

DECK USED:

CARD(S) PULLED:

YOUR INTERPRETATION:

BOOK INTERPRETATION:

"If the plan doesn't work, change the plan, but never the goal."

– Author Unknown

MONDAY	TUESDAY	WEDNESDAY	THURSDAY
31			
3	4	5	6
10	11	12	13
17	18	19	20
24 / 31	25	26	27

Calendar Key

Full Moon

New Moon

 First Quarter

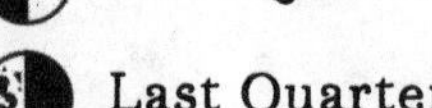 Last Quarter

 Eclipse

 Sun

FRIDAY	SATURDAY	SUNDAY
	1	♑ 2
7	8	♈ 9
14	15	16
21	22	23
28	29	30

JAN

goals

JANUARY

M	T	W	T	F	S	S
27	28	29	30	31	1	2
3	4	5	6	7	8	9
10	11	12	13	14	15	16
17	18	19	20	21	22	23
24	25	26	27	28	29	30
31	1	2	3	4	5	6

GOALS & DREAMS

6-MONTH PROJECT LIST

GOAL: ______________________________ DUE DATE: __________

ENVISION YOUR LIFE AFTER OBTAINING YOUR GOAL.
HOW DO YOU FEEL?

MONTHLY ACTION STEPS:

NOTES:

RITUAL PLANNER

GOAL/INTENTION:

ITEMS NEEDED:

STEPS:

LUNAR PHASES

JANUARY 2ND: NEW MOON IN CAPRICORN

The moon in Capricorn has an emotional seriousness, a sober orientation, and a practical awareness that brings with it a need to feel useful. Using the energies of the new moon and amplified ambitions of Capricorn, this is an ideal time to start new projects.

JANUARY 9TH: FIRST QUARTER IN ARIES

The moon in Aries is emotionally direct and impulsive, with strong, influential feelings. Time for a fresh start, learning new behaviors, establishing new habits. Just don't rush to make decisions, as Aries is apt to do, feeling as though quicker is better. It's not. Take your time to consider what you need, what you want, and choose carefully. The choices made in Aries set the tone for the extended future.

JANUARY 17TH: FULL MOON IN CANCER

The Moon in Cancer instills in you emotional security and a sense of belonging, a sense of nurturing you feel instinctively. You find that you're longing for an intimate connection that's meaningful and long-lasting, enough so you can establish a sense of belonging-put down roots, a place to bunker down as the Universe throws its' trials and tribulations at you. Using the Full Moon energies to work a self-love spell may help to satisfy this desire.

JANUARY 25TH: LAST QUARTER IN SCORPIO

Scorpio energy encourages us to explore our feelings more deeply, and we find we're drawn to sex, power and money. Learning what gets other people going is arousing. Instinctive orientation is to start over from scratch. Only by destroying the roots of disturbances can you begin healing.

JANUARY HERB GUIDE

You will see that there is an Herb Planting Guide section for each month of 2022. The articles cover a range of topics, such as gardening techniques, herb suggestions, and many more. But before I go any further, I want to thank my friend and fellow writer, Kiki Dombrowski, for her help with preparing this guide.

It is thanks to her wise suggestions and creative ideas that I was able to provide you with such an interesting collection of articles. Kiki has been a witch since her teen years, and now writes about witchcraft extensively, including more than five years of writing for Witch Way magazine. Follow Kiki on Twitter at @KiKiD33 or on Instagram at @kikiscauldron.

While witchcraft and nature go hand in hand, it doesn't mean that all witches are expert gardeners, so that is why the first couple of articles of the Herb Planting Guide are covering beginner basics- to give beginners a helping hand and experienced gardeners a refresher. This month is a simple list of common gardening terms.

Common Gardening Terms

Annual: a plant that completes its lifecycle in one year or less
Biennial: a plant that lives for 2 years.
Companion Planting: the practice of using a specific combination of plants growing together in order to provide a variety of benefits (i.e., attract pollinators, deter pests, etc.).
Compost: decomposed organic matter. (See March planting guide for more information)
Deadheading: removing a bloom past its' prime from the plant to encourage new growth
Direct Sow: planting the seed directly into the final growth location
Full Sun: a minimum of 6 hours of direct sunlight
Hardiness Zone: the US was grouped into sections and designated hardiness zone numbers based on climatic conditions to determine which plants will grow best in which areas of the country. To assess your Hardiness Zone, refer to the Hardiness Zone map in the Appendix.
Part Sun/Shade: 3-6 hours of sun a day
Perennial: a plant that lives 2 or more years

A TRUE RESET

It is the beginning of the year. What does this mean? Well, it means a lot of lofty goals, financial recouping from the holiday season, and shaking off the buzz of many events and social obligations.

A new year means that we can finally breathe again. While many websites, listicles, and magazines will tell you now is the time to kick it into gear with a new workout plan, a stricter budget, and new routines, we're going to be that friend that goes... hey witch, slow your roll. While yes, if you are feeling motivated, that's amazing. Work that flow and go with what you feel. However, I would feel like a bad friend if I didn't also gently remind you of the chaotic holiday season that you just went through. Indulge in a bit of self-care this January before you take on the year of 2022.

You may be thinking, "Oh great! Another article on taking a bubble bath. Pass." No, no, hear me out. While yes, if you think I'm not about to tell you to go take a bubble bath, you are crazy. Still, I'm also going to include some other ideas to make an actual refreshing start to your year and help you breathe a little easier. Let's talk about 3 fundamental aspects of your life that tend to get bogged down; your body, mind, and space.

Let's talk about your space.

A cluttered space makes us feel like we're spiraling. It is my own guilty habit, and it often makes me feel overwhelmed and out of control. So I'm going to give you a little homework to schedule into this planner. It will take no more than 30 minutes. Throw out all of those holiday leftovers. I know you're so sure that you're going to do something with that ham bone... but really... are you?

Next, you see that pile of gifts that have no home yet? I know you have no idea if you even like the lamp from Aunt Jo or the slow cooker from your mom that she also gave you a year ago. Take 20 minutes to go through them, give them homes, or decide if they need to be donated.

Finally, now is the perfect time to remove the holiday-specific items from your space. The tree, the Santa decor, and your ironic ugly Christmas sweater for office parties are more than ready to be put away.

Let's talk about your mind.

We've just been through a pretty hectic, though fun season. Parties, feasts, social events often clutter the holiday season, and sometimes we can feel a little overwhelmed. Try a few of these tasks to help unclutter the mind as you go into the new year. Spend about 45 minutes and clean up your inbox. Yes, the dreaded inbox. Deleted everything that is no longer useful and finally respond to the items you've been putting off. Clear out your DVR - yes, you've been recording all 7 seasons of Buffy, but if you've gone almost 3 months without watching a single episode, it's time for it to go. Finally, let us talk about emotions. The holiday season is full of complex emotional situations, and worrying about what your friend meant precisely when she made that comment or why your long-hated cousin was invited to a party, won't do you any good. Let's face it, you won't find answers. People are complicated. Let that shit go.

Let's talk about your body.

This is typically what we associate with self-care. First off, start the year off with a health check. If you are lucky enough to have insurance, get a physical. If not, take stock of any pains, discomforts, and other aspects of your body you may be concerned about.

Next, take about 15 minutes and treat yourself to a Guided Body Scan. This is a beautiful meditation. You can find multiple versions online, which will help you become more intuned with your body.

Now... I know you've been waiting for this part... destressing. Take some time for yourself to do acts of de-stress. Baths, face masks, grounding, meditation - whatever it is that makes you feel clear from tension and stress.

There we go witches, I hope this gives you a little extra motivation to begin the year off with a tabula rasa.

PAUSE & REFLECT

Take a moment and predict what you think this year will be like for you.

JANUARY FESTIVALS

In Benin, starting on the 10th of January, the country honors its ancestors and gods by celebrating the African spirituality, Vodoun (Voodoo). The holiday is celebrated across the whole country, but Ouidah is the epicenter of the festivities. The Fête du Vodoun, or the Vodoun Festival, is a beautiful way to celebrate a spirituality that has traveled world-wide, survived generations, and shaped communities far and wide. The festivities begin with the sacrificial slaughter of a goat to honor the spirits, and followed by joyous dancing, singing, and imbibing of liquor – particularly gin.

[Source: https://en.wikipedia.org/wiki/Fête_du_Vodoun]

USE THE SPACE BELOW TO RECORD YOUR JANUARY CELEBRATIONS

27 DECEMBER
MONDAY

28 DECEMBER
TUESDAY

31 DECEMBER
FRIDAY

1 JANUARY
SATURDAY

29 DECEMBER
WEDNESDAY

30 DECEMBER
THURSDAY

2 JANUARY
SUNDAY

JANUARY - 2022

	M	T	W	T	F	S	S
52	27	28	29	30	31	1	2
1	3	4	5	6	7	8	9
2	10	11	12	13	14	15	16
3	17	18	19	20	21	22	23
4	24	25	26	27	28	29	30
5	31	1	2	3	4	5	6

3 JANUARY
MONDAY

4 JANUARY
TUESDAY

7 JANUARY
FRIDAY

8 JANUARY
SATURDAY

5 JANUARY
WEDNESDAY

6 JANUARY
THURSDAY

9 JANUARY
SUNDAY

JANUARY - 2022

	M	T	W	T	F	S	S
52	27	28	29	30	31	1	2
1	3	4	5	6	7	8	9
2	10	11	12	13	14	15	16
3	17	18	19	20	21	22	23
4	24	25	26	27	28	29	30
5	31	1	2	3	4	5	6

10 JANUARY
MONDAY

11 JANUARY
TUESDAY

14 JANUARY
FRIDAY

15 JANUARY
SATURDAY

12 JANUARY WEDNESDAY

13 JANUARY THURSDAY

16 JANUARY SUNDAY

JANUARY - 2022

	M	T	W	T	F	S	S
52	27	28	29	30	31	1	2
1	3	4	5	6	7	8	9
2	10	11	12	13	14	15	16
3	17	18	19	20	21	22	23
4	24	25	26	27	28	29	30
5	31	1	2	3	4	5	6

17 JANUARY
MONDAY

18 JANUARY
TUESDAY

21 JANUARY
FRIDAY

22 JANUARY
SATURDAY

19 JANUARY
WEDNESDAY

20 JANUARY
THURSDAY

23 JANUARY
SUNDAY

JANUARY - 2022

	M	T	W	T	F	S	S
52	27	28	29	30	31	1	2
1	3	4	5	6	7	8	9
2	10	11	12	13	14	15	16
3	17	18	19	20	21	22	23
4	24	25	26	27	28	29	30
5	31	1	2	3	4	5	6

24 JANUARY
MONDAY

25 JANUARY
TUESDAY

28 JANUARY
FRIDAY

29 JANUARY
SATURDAY

26 JANUARY
WEDNESDAY

27 JANUARY
THURSDAY

30 JANUARY
SUNDAY

JANUARY - 2022

	M	T	W	T	F	S	S
52	27	28	29	30	31	1	2
1	3	4	5	6	7	8	9
2	10	11	12	13	14	15	16
3	17	18	19	20	21	22	23
4	24	25	26	27	28	29	30
5	31	1	2	3	4	5	6

GRATITUDE LIST

MONTHLY TO-DO'S

TRY SOMETHING NEW

CRYSTALS: amethyst

A stone I'd recommend to anyone whether they're new to crystal magic or have been working with crystals for decades, has been valued by cultures all over the world for centuries. Amethyst expands your higher mind, improves psychic ability, intuition, and enhances creativity, logical thinking, passion, and, ironically, temperance and sobriety.

Keep a cluster on your desk to improve your work environment, wear it around your neck to keep your mood light and easy, scatter tumbled stones of amethyst around your altar to enhance rituals, or add chips or beads of amethyst to satchels for spells. Fades in direct sunlight – to cleanse energies or clean the stone just hold under running water.

Source: https://www.crystalvaults.com/crystal-encyclopedia/amethyst

CARD SPREAD

Card 1: Past - Card 2 : Present - Card 3: Future

SPELL: lost items

This spell originated in Greece, and all you need is a handkerchief or scarf– natural fabrics work best, i.e.. cotton, wool, silk –some soil, and visualization skills! First, visualize the item clearly as possible while holding the kerchief. With the item pictured in your mind, tie the fabric into a knot. Take it out to your garden or over to a potted plant and say "Back to the earth, back to the ground. I won't untie you until you are found." Press the knotted scarf/ handkerchief into the soil and leave it undisturbed until you find the lost item. When you find what was lost, untie the handkerchief, launder it and put it away.

ENTITY

Create an ancestor altar by creating a clean space with water, photos, and loved vices.

SELF-CARE

Go for a walk. For real. 5 minutes. 30 minutes. Just do it.

TEA: gunpowder green

From the Guangdong province of China. Gunpowder tea is made up of leaves hand-rolled into tiny pellets. Mix with peppermint to create "Moroccan Mint" tea.

HERBS: rosemary

Rosemary is truly an epic herb, because it can be used as a substitution for literally any herb that spells or rituals may call for. Fresh rosemary is great for potions and cooking magic, while dried rosemary can be burned as incense, added to a sachet, or ground to dress a candle. It possesses several metaphysical properties, including but not limited to: protection, prosperity, healing, banishment, love, luck, psychic powers, and personal power.

Record a Card Pull

DECK USED:

CARD(S) PULLED:

YOUR INTERPRETATION:

BOOK INTERPRETATION:

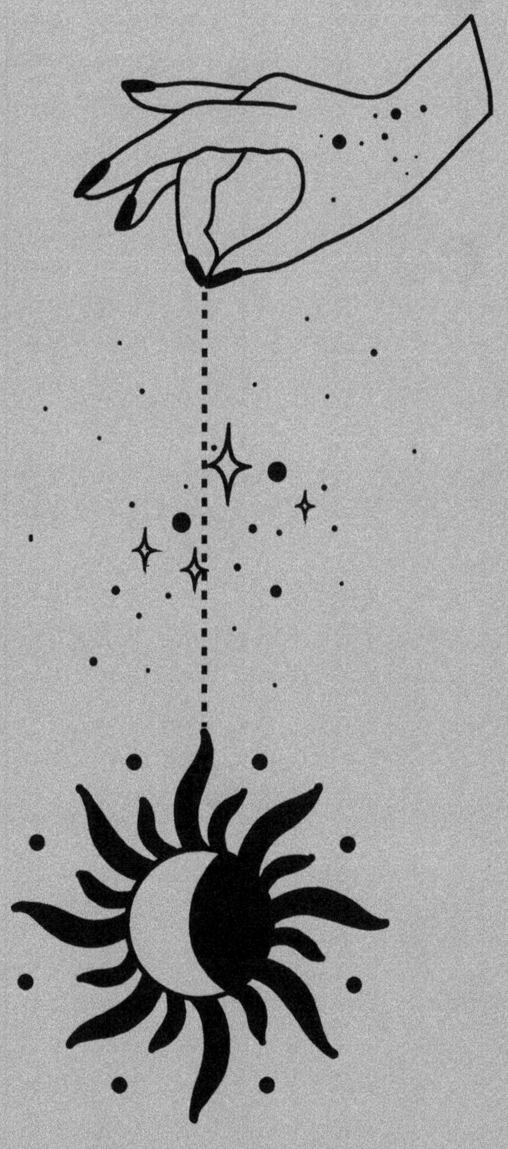

"The true secret of happiness lies in the taking a genuine interest in all the details of daily life."

– William Morris

MONDAY	TUESDAY	WEDNESDAY	THURSDAY
31	Imbolc 1	2	3
7	8	9	10
14	15	16	17
21	22	23	24
28			

Calendar Key

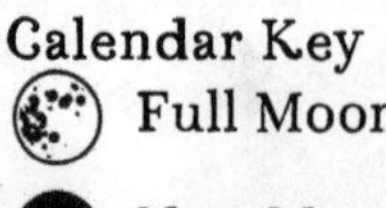

Full Moon

New Moon

First Quarter

Last Quarter

Eclipse

Sun

FRIDAY	SATURDAY	SUNDAY
4	5	6
11	12	13
18	☉♓ 19	20
25	26	27

FEB

goals

FEBRUARY

M	T	W	T	F	S	S
31	1	2	3	4	5	6
7	8	9	10	11	12	13
14	15	16	17	18	19	20
21	22	23	24	25	26	27
28	1	2	3	4	5	6

LUNAR PHASES

FEBRUARY 1ST: NEW MOON IN AQUARIUS

The moon in Aquarius gives us the need for emotional freedoms which can cause complications in our relationships. Can also be a time when you are able to better understand your emotions, freeing you from negative feelings such as jealousy, fear, and anger.

FEBRUARY 8TH: FIRST QUARTER IN TAURUS

Your sense of safety arises from the need for stability which is difficult to find at the moment. The key to stability is acceptance - accepting that change is a part of life, and acceptance of who you are as a person. When you accept yourself you will find that peace and tranquility are much easier to come by in your daily life.

FEBRUARY 16TH: FULL MOON IN LEO

Impressing others and receiving praise will give you a sense of safety and sevurity while the moon is in Leo. This only sets you up for failure, as you'll find yourself at a loss as soon as you're put in the spotlight. The key to navigating through Leo is accepting that feedback and criticism are useful, they help you improve. The first step to accepting these facts is to admit you are afraid of criticism, and to admit that you can't accept criticism. Only once you admit the truth of the problem can you work through it.

FEBRUARY 23RD: LAST QUARTER IN SCORPIO

Scorpio energy encourages us to explore our feelings more deeply and helps us evaluate things in our life more objectively. This time is best utilized to move away from that which no longer serves, especially when it comes to shallow relationships that aren't beneficial for the parties involved.

RITUAL PLANNER

GOAL/INTENTION:

ITEMS NEEDED:

STEPS:

FEBRUARY HERBS

Gardening can be relatively simple- it's a matter of caring and crooning to plants. It becomes quite vexing if you don't thoughtfully plan your garden and end up with sick and/or dying plants. Choose the plants you wish to grow, keeping in mind the Hardiness Zone, sun exposure and soil type.

Next you'll determine the gardening method, (See July Herb Planting Guide for more information about garden layouts), where in your yard the garden will go, and then design the garden. Each plant is unique, so a major part of gardening is taking the time to learn about each one. It's important to remember your plants are living beings that crave love, support, encouragement, and attention.

HERB	SIZE/ SPREAD	START SEEDS IN-SIDE/OUTSIDE	HARDINESS ZONE	NATIVE REGION	GROWTH TYPE**	SUN/- SOIL*
Cilantro/ Coriander	12"2'/2"-1.5'	Direct Sow in Fall	8-10	Southern Europe, Western Mediterranean	A	FS/WD
Chives	12-18"	8-10 after/3-4 before	3-10	Temperate areas of Europe, Asia, North America	P	FS/RM
Lemon Balm	12-24"/12-24"	8 before-last frost	4-9	South-central Europe, Mediterranean Basin, Iran, Central Asia	P	FS/WD- S
Sage	12-48"-30"	6-10 before/1-2 before	5-8	Mediterraneean	P	FS/WD
*Weeks before or afer last spring frost						
** A=Annual P=Perennial						
** FS= full sun, PS= partial sun; WD= well-drained, M= moist, RM, rich moint, L= loamy, LS=loamy/sandy						

THE MAGIC OF SEX

Rather than fretting over flowers and hearts and romance this month, why not focus instead on a rather enjoyable way to express love: sex. The magic of sex comes from the orgasm- the climax, that release of built-up energy. This can be sex with yourself, a partner- multiple partners even. Sex can be an amazing part of your adult life. As witches, we can utilize the energy of our orgasms in our magic.

When you work a spell, you build up the energy, right? And when you reach that peak and are at the height of the working, you release that energy in a burst. It's not unlike sex when the pleasure of the stimulation increases and increases until you reach your climax – your orgasm.

With sex magick, all you need is to reach orgasm, and you can change your world...
~Damon Brand, Adventures in Sex Magick

It doesn't take much – as I said, a partner isn't necessary. You can work spells just as efficiently when you pleasure yourself. The release of the energy is often carried out with your orgasm, but for those of you who have yet to experience one, don't worry. Even you can work sex magic. Just spending time exploring ways to pleasure yourself can raise energy to be directed towards a working.

All you need to work sex magic is yourself and the ability to visualize your intent. You can ritualize the practice if you wish, but it's not necessary. Whatever you are comfortable doing. I personally didn't build a ritual at first, as it took time for me to acclimate myself to concentrate on manifesting what I wanted while maintaining my arousal and stimulating myself in the way I needed to in order to come. As you begin having sex, or masturbating, see yourself, your day-to-day life, as you think it would be once your desire has manifested. As your arousal increases, and the intensity of the love-making (again, whether it's with yourself or another) intensifies, explore the potential future deeper – the details more precise, more refined, and when you feel that build of energy, and the climb to the orgasm, concentrate on what you're bringing into your life- the job, the money, the new home, whatever it is. When you orgasm, feel the built-up energy release, surfing the waves of your pleasure out into the universe to manifest your desire.

PAUSE & REFLECT

If you could get advice from a fictional witch, who would it be? What would you ask them?

FEBRUARY FESTIVALS

For the first two weeks of February every year, Easter Island carries out the Tapati Rapa Nui Festival. This cultural festival was established in the 1970's in order to maintain and promote the Rapa Nui culture, helping to generate interest and a 'sense of identity' in people, especially kids. From February 1st to the 15th, the island is abuzz with competitions, singing, dancing, and a number of sporting events. One remarkable sporting event they have is haka pei, where you sit on a banana tree trunk and slide down the island's steepest slope. Each event carries a certain number of points, which are used in the competition for the Queen of Tapati. Two women are selected as candidates, and they compete in each of the sporting events - Haka Pei, the island triathlon, swimming, canoeing, and horse racing. The woman with the most points at the end is crowned Queen. [Source: easterislandspirit.com]

USE THE SPACE BELOW TO RECORD YOUR FEBRUARY CELEBRATIONS

GRATITUDE LIST

MONTHLY TO-DO'S

TRY SOMETHING NEW

Crystals aren't used by all witches, so don't feel you have to go out and buy a bunch. I believe that, should one benefit from using crystals, the crystals will find you. You may see a crystal cluster at a craft store, or perhaps you're drawn to tumbled stones at your local occult shop. When it comes to collecting crystals, follow your instincts. Should your first choice be too pricey, follow your gut to the next best choice. When you start to collect crystals, get or make a nice cloth bag, or pretty little box to keep them in while they're not being used.

CARD SPREAD
Card 1: Today's Emotion - Card 2: Today's Action - Card 3: Today's Goal

SPELL: Pumpkin Seed Prosperity Spell
My 5 year old son came up with this, but I use it whenever I have an unexpected bill or want to treat myself and need a little extra cash. I use a plastic egg (like the kind you get for Ostara/Easter), but any little container will do. Inside the container put a pumpkin seed, three silver coins, and a bay leaf.

As you put the ingredients inside think about how much money you need and when you need it by. Keep the egg/container by your desk or stick it in your car. When you get the money requested, donate the coins (I typically put them in a charity box for kids or animal shelter at the gas station check-out counter), bury the pumpkin seed and bay leaf, and put the egg/container away. Be sure to thank the items and release the energy to bless someone else in need.

ENTITY
Create a routine of speaking out loud to the spirits weekly, and eventually daily.

SELF-CARE
Not all books need to be for growth and development. Read some erotica.

TEA: Chai Tea
Blend black tea with dried orange peel, cinnamon, and clove to make an easy and delicious chai blend.

HERBS: Vervain
Vervain, specifically verbena officinalis (native to Europe), has been prized for its magical properties and uses since the Iron Age, when the ancient Druids used vervain to bless Bards, in rituals as offerings, or ingested to aid with spiritual communication or pathworking. Vervain helps with psychic work, memory, spirit work, protection, and purification.

31 JANUARY
MONDAY

1 FEBRUARY
TUESDAY

4 FEBRUARY
FRIDAY

5 FEBRUARY
SATURDAY

2 FEBRUARY
WEDNESDAY

3 FEBRUARY
THURSDAY

6 FEBRUARY
SUNDAY

FEBRUARY - 2022

	M	T	W	T	F	S	S
5	31	1	2	3	4	5	6
6	7	8	9	10	11	12	13
7	14	15	16	17	18	19	20
8	21	22	23	24	25	26	27
9	28	1	2	3	4	5	6

7 FEBRUARY
MONDAY

8 FEBRUARY
TUESDAY

11 FEBRUARY
FRIDAY

12 FEBRUARY
SATURDAY

9 FEBRUARY
WEDNESDAY

10 FEBRUARY
THURSDAY

13 FEBRUARY
SUNDAY

FEBRUARY - 2022

	M	T	W	T	F	S	S
5	31	1	2	3	4	5	6
6	7	8	9	10	11	12	13
7	14	15	16	17	18	19	20
8	21	22	23	24	25	26	27
9	28	1	2	3	4	5	6

14 FEBRUARY
MONDAY

15 FEBRUARY
TUESDAY

18 FEBRUARY
FRIDAY

19 FEBRUARY
SATURDAY

16 FEBRUARY
WEDNESDAY

17 FEBRUARY
THURSDAY

20 FEBRUARY
SUNDAY

FEBRUARY - 2022

	M	T	W	T	F	S	S
5	31	1	2	3	4	5	6
6	7	8	9	10	11	12	13
7	14	15	16	17	18	19	20
8	21	22	23	24	25	26	27
9	28	1	2	3	4	5	6

21 FEBRUARY
MONDAY

22 FEBRUARY
TUESDAY

25 FEBRUARY
FRIDAY

26 FEBRUARY
SATURDAY

23 FEBRUARY
WEDNESDAY

24 FEBRUARY
THURSDAY

27 FEBRUARY
SUNDAY

FEBRUARY - 2022

	M	T	W	T	F	S	S
5	31	1	2	3	4	5	6
6	7	8	9	10	11	12	13
7	14	15	16	17	18	19	20
8	21	22	23	24	25	26	27
9	28	1	2	3	4	5	6

Record a Card Pull

DECK USED:

CARD(S) PULLED:

YOUR INTERPRETATION:

BOOK INTERPRETATION:

“A Witch is born out of the true hungers of her time.”

- Ray Bradbury

MONDAY	TUESDAY	WEDNESDAY	THURSDAY
	1	2	3
7	8	9	10
14	15	16	17
21	22	23	24
28	29	30	31

Calendar Key

Full Moon

First Quarter

Eclipse

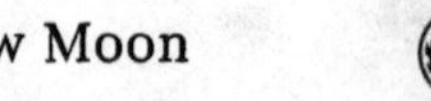

New Moon

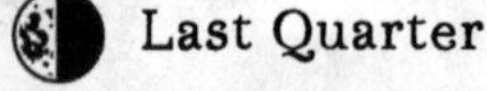

Last Quarter

Sun

MAR

FRIDAY	SATURDAY	SUNDAY
4	5	6
11	12	13
♍ 18	19	Spring Equinox/Ostara 20
♑ 25	26	27

goals

MARCH

M	T	W	T	F	S	S
28	1	2	3	4	5	6
7	8	9	10	11	12	13
14	15	16	17	18	19	20
21	22	23	24	25	26	27
28	29	30	31	1	2	3

LUNAR PHASES

MARCH 2ND: NEW MOON IN PISCES

The moon in Pisces is a great time for a creative or spiritual quest, as the energy heightens your emotional sensitivity and perception of your surroundings. Be mindful of feelings of insecurity. Should you begin to feel insecure just be patient and open to letting events unfold as they come.

MARCH 10TH: FIRST QUARTER IN GEMINI

Under the Gemini moon you may find that communicating your feelings and emotions becomes easier. Your actions are motivated by the desire for variety and the urge to satisfy curiosity. Just be careful you don't become reckless and fickle – the key is harmony of the mind and heart.

MARCH 18TH: FULL MOON IN VIRGO

The Virgo moon is one of order and practicality. You feel you have to reorganize and bring order to anything you feel is in chaos. This can lead to being intolerant of others, so try focusing more on solving problems, creating order within your life, and helping others without judgement.

MARCH 25TH: LAST QUARTER IN CAPRICORN

The moon in Capricorn has an emotional seriousness, a sober orientation, and a practical awareness that brings with it a need to feel useful. Using the energies of the new moon and amplified ambitions of Capricorn, this is an ideal time to start new projects.

RITUAL PLANNER

GOAL/INTENTION:

ITEMS NEEDED:

STEPS:

MARCH HERB PLANTING GUIDE: DIY COMPOST

Compost, simply put, is decomposed organic material. You could buy compost, but making your own homemade compost saves money, supports the environment, and provides your garden with nutrients infused with your positive energies. According to the EPA website, composting requires three basic ingredients: Browns, Greens, and Water. Browns provide carbon and consist of things like dead leaves, twigs, branches. Greens provide nitrogen, consisting of things like grass clippings, tea bags coffee grounds, eggshells, fruit scraps, and vegetable waste. Add enough water to make the material moist, which helps break down the organic matter. The compost should have an equal amount of browns to greens, and the layers should alternate between organic matter and different-sized particles.

You'll need a plastic bin with a lid. The recommended size is 18 gallons or larger. Drill 8-10 holes 1-2" apart in the bottom of the bin and in the lid. Put first bin inside a second bin if you want to collect and save the liquid (aka compost tea) leaking from the bottom of the first. Decide where the compost bin will be kept (on the porch, outside the kitchen window, in a shed, next to the garden, etc) and get it into position. You'll add the material in layers, adding water between each layer to moisten any dry material. Lay down the base material, ie. shredded newspaper, dried leaves, until the bin is about a quarter of the way full. Add dirt until the bin is about half full. Add scraps and other compostable material. Make sure the scraps are small in size to make decomposition easier - cut up the food scraps, rinse and crush the egg shells, tear up the napkins and paper towels.

With a small shovel stir the contents, folding them into each other. Make sure the compost is moist but not soggy and secure the lid. Every day the bin should be shaken up a bit to make sure air is flowing through the entire bin. If it's too moist, add shredded leaves, sawdust, or newspaper to soak up excess water. Alternatively, if the material is too dry, use a spray bottle to dampen the material. Keep a bin or bag in the kitchen to collect food scraps that you'll add to the compost bin every week or so, along with twigs and leaves and such to maintain the green to brown ratio. Compost will be ready in 2-3 months. You'll know it's ready because it will be a soft, dark, soil-like material. Use it as mulch or mix with soil to fertilize your garden.

Resources:
https://www.epa.gov/recycle/composting-home
https://www.thespruce.com/compost-bin-from-plastic-storage-container-2539493
https://www.younghouselove.com/younghouselovedotcompost/

MAGIC FOR GOALS

Hey witch! So by now, you've probably filled out your goal sheets, and you've figured out all the practical steps that it will take to get there. This is by far one of the most important steps it takes to create and obtain goals. Knowing step by step how to get there gives you a practical guide to getting where you need to be. I want to provide you with today a few magical ideas that you can use to help add power and magic to your goal.

You will need the following:
-A small charm bag
-A few drops of cinnamon oil
-A bay leaf
-A slice of fresh ginger
-A pinch of red clover

First: Go about creating your space as you usually do; cleanse, bathe, prepare the area and yourself.

Second: What is the next upcoming milestone for your goal? What do you need to obtain or accomplish? Writing the proposal? Saving the money? Accomplishing the task? Whatever it is, write the next milestone on your bay leaf. Carefully then anoint the bay leaf with your cinnamon oil as your focus on successfully completing your milestone.

Third: Sprinkle your red clover into your charm bag before placing the bay leaf inside. Finally, place your piece of ginger into the bag and close tightly.

Fourth: Keep this charm bag with you on your person until you complete your milestone. Your pocket, your bra, your purse, or your wallet. It must remain close to you and within your focus until the milestone is completed.

Once the milestone is finished, you can dispose of your bag and then create a new one for the next.

Wishing you all the success and luck as your work to complete your goals, witches.

PAUSE & REFLECT

If you could cast a spell and get instant results, what would you cast? and why?

MARCH FESTIVALS

One of the most celebrated festivals in India is Holi. Holi is an enthusiastically celebrated ancient Hindu festival that lasts for a day and a night. The lighting of the ritual bon fire the night before signifies the start to the festival the following day, serving as a symbol of the triumph of good over evil. Holi is about respect, love, and friendship. Holi is known as the Festival of Colors, named for the tradition of 'playing with colors', when adults and children alike gather in the streets to smear vibrantly colored gulal on one another and splash each other with brightly colored water, or throw water balloons filled with colored water at each other. In addition to playing with colors, Holi is celebrated by dancing, singing, eating of sweets, giving of gifts, and honoring of the gods.
[Source: https://www.holifestival.org/festival-of-colours.html]

USE THE SPACE BELOW TO RECORD YOUR MARCH CELEBRATIONS

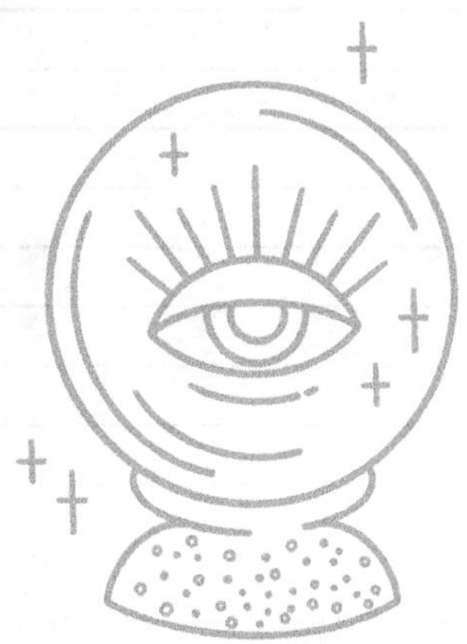

28 FEBRUARY
MONDAY

1 MARCH
TUESDAY

4 MARCH
FRIDAY

5 MARCH
SATURDAY

2 MARCH
WEDNESDAY

3 MARCH
THURSDAY

6 MARCH
SUNDAY

MARCH - 2022

	M	T	W	T	F	S	S
9	28	1	2	3	4	5	6
10	7	8	9	10	11	12	13
11	14	15	16	17	18	19	20
12	21	22	23	24	25	26	27
13	28	29	30	31	1	2	3

7 MARCH
MONDAY

8 MARCH
TUESDAY

11 MARCH
FRIDAY

12 MARCH
SATURDAY

9 MARCH
WEDNESDAY

10 MARCH
THURSDAY

13 MARCH
SUNDAY

MARCH - 2022

	M	T	W	T	F	S	S
9	28	1	2	3	4	5	6
10	7	8	9	10	11	12	13
11	14	15	16	17	18	19	20
12	21	22	23	24	25	26	27
13	28	29	30	31	1	2	3

14 MARCH
MONDAY

15 MARCH
TUESDAY

18 MARCH
FRIDAY

19 MARCH
SATURDAY

16 MARCH
WEDNESDAY

17 MARCH
THURSDAY

20 MARCH
SUNDAY

MARCH - 2022

	M	T	W	T	F	S	S
9	28	1	2	3	4	5	6
10	7	8	9	10	11	12	13
11	14	15	16	17	18	19	20
12	21	22	23	24	25	26	27
13	28	29	30	31	1	2	3

21 MARCH
MONDAY

22 MARCH
TUESDAY

25 MARCH
FRIDAY

26 MARCH
SATURDAY

23 MARCH
WEDNESDAY

24 MARCH
THURSDAY

27 MARCH
SUNDAY

MARCH - 2022

	M	T	W	T	F	S	S
9	28	1	2	3	4	5	6
10	7	8	9	10	11	12	13
11	14	15	16	17	18	19	20
12	21	22	23	24	25	26	27
13	28	29	30	31	1	2	3

28 MARCH
MONDAY

29 MARCH
TUESDAY

1 APRIL
FRIDAY

2 APRIL
SATURDAY

30 MARCH
WEDNESDAY

31 MARCH
THURSDAY

3 APRIL
SUNDAY

MARCH - 2022

	M	T	W	T	F	S	S
9	28	1	2	3	4	5	6
10	7	8	9	10	11	12	13
11	14	15	16	17	18	19	20
12	21	22	23	24	25	26	27
13	28	29	30	31	1	2	3

GRATITUDE LIST

MONTHLY TO-DO'S

TRY SOMETHING NEW

CRYSTALS: Malachite
Malachite is a stone of protection, using earthy energies to absorb and cleanse negative energies and pollutants. This stone has an incredible grounding effect, the dark green colors and swirls representing the beauty of flora. It has been said that this stone is excellent for easing the fear of flying, and is often used by pilots and airline attendants.

CARD SPREAD
1: What You Know - Card 2: What you are doing - Card 3: What you need to know

SPELL: Travel Protection Sachet
Inspired by Scott Cunningham's' Travel Protection Sachet. To keep your vehicle safe, or to protect yourself (and your family) during vacation, this small, but potent, sachet will ensure you return home safe and sound.

You'll need black (protection) cloth and yellow (travel) thread (or vice versa), a small amethyst, and equal parts dragons' blood resin (or cinnamon, both add potency to any spell), comfrey and basil. Put the amethyst in the pouch, sprinkle the herbs on top, all the while envisioning yourself leaving and returning, safe and sound. If you wish, you can recite an incantation, such as "A stone of purple, and herbs times three I put in, I empower this sachet to protect my vehicle and all within. Deliver me to, deliver me fro, I'll be safe wherever I go." When the ingredients are all inside stitch up the top side, sealing the pouch closed. When you place the sachet in your car, envision a white or yellow light shining from the sachet, growing and growing until your vehicle is encompassed by sphere of protective light. Recharge as needed (i.e. once a month, at the turn of the season, however often you feel called to do so)

ENTITY
Leave an offering of your loved one's favorite food at your altar, then dispose at a crossroads.

SELF-CARE
Watch that weird, guilty pleasure movie that only you like.

TEA: Silver Needle Tea
Silver Needle is one of the most beloved Chinese teas, produced in the Fujian province. It is only collected during a few days in early spring.

HERBS
Meeting the spirit of your plants is an incredible experience, as the herbs can offer helpful hints regarding growth and care, as well as magical uses. Sit with the herb nearby, close your eyes and enter a meditative state with the intention of connecting with the herbs' spirit. The spirit may appear to you in human form, as colors, in the shape of the plant - it varies. When you feel you have made a connection, ask what name you should call the spirit, introduce yourself, and converse for a few minutes. Keep a journal of your experiences.

APRIL FESTIVALS

The Parrtjima (parr-chee-ma) Festival in Alice Springs Australia is a free 10-day event that uses the newest technology to celebrate the world's oldest living culture, making this authentic Aboriginal festival is the only one of its' kind. The Arrernte people of Alice Springs host the Parrtjima Festival to display their artwork and, more importantly, educate people about their culture. During the day, visitors are encouraged to immerse themselves in the schedule of events, participating in interactive workshops, attending talks and discussions, viewing art created by local artists. The energies transform after night fall, as the mountains become illuminated by vibrant light shows, and live music echoes across the desert while people dance and celebrate. [Source: https://www.australia.com/en-us/events/arts-culture-and-music/parrtjima-festival.html]

USE THE SPACE BELOW TO RECORD YOUR APRIL CELEBRATIONS

"Even a happy life cannot be without a measure of darkness, and the word happy would lose its meaning if it were not balanced by sadness. It is far better to take things as they come along with patience and equanimity."

-Carl Jung

MONDAY	TUESDAY	WEDNESDAY	THURSDAY
28	29	30	31
4	5	6	7
11	12	13	14
18	19	☀ ♉ 20	21
25	26	27	28

Calendar Key

Full Moon

New Moon

First Quarter

Last Quarter

Eclipse

Sun

FRIDAY	SATURDAY	SUNDAY
♈ 1	2	3
8	♋ 9	10
15	♎ 16	17
22	♒ 23	24
29	♉ 30	

APR

goals

APRIL

M	T	W	T	F	S	S
28	29	30	31	1	2	3
4	5	6	7	8	9	10
11	12	13	14	15	16	17
18	19	20	21	22	23	24
25	26	27	28	29	30	1

LUNAR PHASES

APRIL 1ST: NEW MOON IN ARIES

The moon in Aries is emotionally direct and impulsive, with strong, influential feelings. Time for a fresh start, learning new behaviors, establishing new habits. Just don't rush to make decisions, as Aries is apt to do, feeling as though quicker is better. It's not. Take your time to consider what you need, what you want, and choose carefully. The choices made in Aries set the tone for the extended future.

APRIL 9TH: FIRST QUARTER IN CANCER

The Moon in Cancer instills in you emotional security and a sense of belonging, a sense of nurturing you feel instinctively. You find that you're longing for an intimate connection that's meaningful and long-lasting, enough so you can establish a sense of belonging- put down roots, a place to bunker down as the Universe throws its' trials and tribulations at you. Using the Full Moon energies to work a self-love spell may help to satisfy this desire.

APRIL 16TH: FULL MOON IN LIBRA

The moon in Libra drives us for a sense of order, but unlike that of the moon in Virgo, we are satisfied by pleasant interactions and aesthetics in the environment. The need for order and harmony are strong, and rather than deal with confrontation you try to keep everything 'nice'. Don't let the Libra moon make you forget who you are, and certainly resist the urge to bottle up your feelings.

APRIL 23RD: LAST QUARTER IN AQUARIUS

The moon in Aquarius gives us the need for emotional freedoms which can cause complications in our relationships. Can also be a time when you are able to better understand your emotions, freeing you from negative feelings such as jealousy, fear, and anger.

APRIL 30TH: NEW MOON IN TAURUS

Your sense of safety arises from the need for stability which is difficult to find at the moment. The key to stability is acceptance - accepting that change is a part of life, and acceptance of who you are as a person. When you accept yourself you will find that peace and tranquility are much easier to come by in your daily life.

RITUAL PLANNER

GOAL/INTENTION:

ITEMS NEEDED:

STEPS:

APRIL HERBS

Elemental gardens are an excellent way to manifest and balance the energies of the four elements. There are a number of ways to call the powers of the elements into your garden. One such way would be to plant herbs associated with each element, such as the herbs in the chart above.

Another method would be for the garden itself to represent Earth, a pinwheel or windchimes for Air, a fountain or rain collection container for Water, and pretty solar lights for Fire. If you have the space, build a path in the shape of a labyrinth into the garden so you may walk the labyrinth meditating upon the four elements.

HERB	SIZE/ SPREAD	START SEEDS INSIDE/OUTSIDE	HARDINESS ZONE	NATIVE REGION	GROWTH TYPE**	SUN SOIL
Chamomile (German)	20-30/ 8-12'	6-8/1-2 before	4-9	US: Northern Colorado to Wisconsin	P	FS/W
Heliotrope	1-4'/ 1-2'	NR/4-6 Before Frost	2-11	Eastern Mediterra-nean Western Asia	P	FS/W
Lavender (English)	18-36/ 24"	4-6/Time of Frost	4-9	Southern Europe Asia Minor Australia parts of US	P	FS/W
Primrose	6-12"/ 6-18"	6-8/Frost	1-11	Eastern Mediterranean Iran Caucasus	A	FS/W
*Weeks before or afer last spring frost						
** A=Annual P=Perennial						
** FS= full sun, PS= partial sun; WD= well-drained, M= moist, RM, rich moint, L= loamy, LS=loamy/sandy						

Properties:
Chamomile: Element- Water. Associated with purification, protection, meditation, and sleep.
Heliotrope: Element- Fire. Named for Greek god of the sun, Helios. The nymph Clytie pined for Helios so deeply she spent all her time sitting and gazing at the sun, not eating or sleeping, so Helios turned her into a flower. She continues to watch the sun from dawn to dusk each day.
Lavender: Element-Air. Considered one of the most valuable herbs that every witch should have.
Primrose: Element- Earth. Often described in folklore as conduit to Otherworld and realm of Faery.

PAUSE & REFLECT

If your life was a book, what would the title be and what would the chapters be named?

DIY CHARMED QUILTED PLANNER COVER

It's finally April! The sun is warm, the landscape is growing greener each day, the birds are chirping and the bees are buzzing. Speaking of bees: the bee is a magnificent creature, and the image of the bee is a great way to manifest productivity, efficiency, and encourage teamwork. You've been working with this planner for a few months now, and it might be starting to show signs of wear. I know my planners start to get crushed corners, warped covers, and the occasional wrinkled page if the planner doesn't have a band or button to keep it closed.

We are going to utilize the creative energies of spring to make a protective cover for our planners that will double as productivity charms! Following the advice and working the magic will take you far, but you'll still fall short of your goals if you're prone to procrastination. A little boost to your productivity will ensure you're using the planner efficiently.

SUPPLIES

- Fabric – recommended cotton or polyester blend. Check out the solid colored 'fat quarter' bundles in craft stores that will be the accent colors, and get a yard or so of bumblebee patterned fabric
- Muslin cloth
- Quilt batting
- Thread
- Sewing supplies- pins, and either hand sewing needles or a sewing machine.

INSTRUCTIONS:

Lay the planner down on the muslin and measure 2.5" from each side and 1" from the top and bottom. Then lay out the batting and cut it to fit the planner. the folded pockets at each side of the cover shouldn't be thick, so you only want the batting to cover the book itself.

Lay out a solid color that will be the lining, then lay the cut muslin over. Pin and cut to same size as the muslin.

This is the fun part- designing the quilt. I will cut the fabric into squares and/or rectangles, then I'll lay them out in a pattern that's appealing over the muslin. Keep seam allowance in mind- so the design before it's sewn will be bigger than the muslin piece - make sure it's at least .75" bigger on all sides, because the final product will be smaller.

Lay the front cover piece down face up. Put the lining piece over it, front side down. Now lay the batting down in the middle, leaving 2.5" of material extending from each side. Lay the muslin over the batting and pin them all into place. You will sew along the top and bottom first, securing the batting in place. Next you'll sew the sides, leaving an 1.5" open on one side so you can turn it right side out. Carefully stitch the hole.

Now lay the cover face side down and fold the sides in to make wide pockets on each side. Stitch in place along the top and bottom. Turn the pockets right side out.

Slide one pocket over the front cover of the planner, then the other pocket over the back cover. And viola, you're done!

If you wish you can add a pocket for pens, a ribbon to serve as a bookmark, or maybe add a button to the front and elastic hook on the back to secure the planner closed. Whenever you look at the bumblebees think about how productive they are, and channel that energy into yourself, your plans, and your magical works.

28 MARCH
MONDAY

29 MARCH
TUESDAY

1 APRIL
FRIDAY

2 APRIL
SATURDAY

30 MARCH
WEDNESDAY

31 MARCH
THURSDAY

3 APRIL
SUNDAY

MARCH - 2022

	M	T	W	T	F	S	S
9	28	1	2	3	4	5	6
10	7	8	9	10	11	12	13
11	14	15	16	17	18	19	20
12	21	22	23	24	25	26	27
13	28	29	30	31	1	2	3

4 APRIL
MONDAY

5 APRIL
TUESDAY

8 APRIL
FRIDAY

9 APRIL
SATURDAY

6 APRIL
WEDNESDAY

7 APRIL
THURSDAY

10 APRIL
SUNDAY

APRIL - 2022

	M	T	W	T	F	S	S
13	28	29	30	31	1	2	3
14	4	5	6	7	8	9	10
15	11	12	13	14	15	16	17
16	18	19	20	21	22	23	24
17	25	26	27	28	29	30	1

11 APRIL
MONDAY

12 APRIL
TUESDAY

15 APRIL
FRIDAY

16 APRIL
SATURDAY

13 APRIL WEDNESDAY

14 APRIL THURSDAY

17 APRIL SUNDAY

APRIL - 2022

	M	T	W	T	F	S	S
13	28	29	30	31	1	2	3
14	4	5	6	7	8	9	10
15	11	12	13	14	15	16	17
16	18	19	20	21	22	23	24
17	25	26	27	28	29	30	1

18 APRIL
MONDAY

19 APRIL
TUESDAY

22 APRIL
FRIDAY

23 APRIL
SATURDAY

20 APRIL
WEDNESDAY

21 APRIL
THURSDAY

24 APRIL
SUNDAY

APRIL - 2022

	M	T	W	T	F	S	S
13	28	29	30	31	1	2	3
14	4	5	6	7	8	9	10
15	11	12	13	14	15	16	17
16	18	19	20	21	22	23	24
17	25	26	27	28	29	30	1

25 APRIL
MONDAY

26 APRIL
TUESDAY

29 APRIL
FRIDAY

30 APRIL
SATURDAY

27 APRIL
WEDNESDAY

28 APRIL
THURSDAY

1 MAY
SUNDAY

APRIL - 2022

	M	T	W	T	F	S	S
13	28	29	30	31	1	2	3
14	4	5	6	7	8	9	10
15	11	12	13	14	15	16	17
16	18	19	20	21	22	23	24
17	25	26	27	28	29	30	1

GRATITUDE LIST

MONTHLY TO-DO'S

TRY SOMETHING NEW

CRYSTALS

Protect your home with a crystal house ward. First, cleanse your home- clean it as you would normally, then use your preferred method for cleansing energies. For the ward you'll need a drawing of your home and four crystals of protection. Suggested crystals: amethyst, black tourmaline, smoky quartz, crystal quartz, obsidian (follow your instinct).

Set one stone in each corner of your home. Go to your altar or sacred space and sit with your drawing. Imagine the crystals at each corner, and 'see' white light of protection emanating from each one, crisscrossing all over your home, creating a sphere of protective energy. Alternatively, you could envision thick vines coming from each crystal, wrapping your home in a thick knot.

Source: Woodfield, Stephanie. (2017). Dark Goddess Craft: A Journey through the heart of transformation. Llewellyn Publications.

CARD SPREAD

Card 1: Conscious - Card 2: Action - Card 3: Unconscious

SPELL

Need a boost of confidence? This glamour spell will do the trick! Take something small, like a piece of jewelry, and hold it in your power hand. Think about yourself behaving as though you were the most confident person in the world. You're giving a speech without a stutter or a bead of sweat, you're standing up to your horrible boss, or you're finally telling your cranky old neighbor to pick up after her dog- whatever it is, see it clearly. Send that image down your spine, into your arm, down and out of your palm and into that object. Visualize the item filling with this energy of confidence. You may wish to say an incantation – When I put on this *item* I'll be confident, I'll be secure, with this on my body I will not demure.

ENTITY

Using 3 paintable masks from a craft store, get artsy and decorate to honor Hecate. Leave out to remind the spirits they are watched over.

SELF-CARE

If you sleep in once in a while the world will not end.

TEA: Bounce Back Tea

Blend green tea, peppermint, cardamom, and marigold to create a tea that will help you recover from sickness.

HERBS

Dragons' Blood, most often taken from the Draconis palm (Dracaena draco), is a crystalline resin that can be added to a sachet, crushed, and added to loose incense, or powdered and used as a candle dressing. Use Dragons blood in workings with the intention of banishing, protection, sexuality, love, money, luck, healing (particularly involving bleeding), or to give a boost to the magic or your personal power. Do not ingest or apply directly to the skin.

Record a Card Pull

DECK USED:

CARD(S) PULLED:

YOUR INTERPRETATION:

BOOK INTERPRETATION:

"The first time I called myself a 'Witch' was the most magical moment of my life."

-Margot Adler

MONDAY	TUESDAY	WEDNESDAY	THURSDAY
30	31		
2	3	4	5
9	10	11	12
16	17	18	19
23 / 30	24 / 31	25	26

Calendar Key

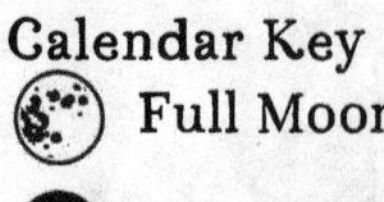
Full Moon

New Moon

First Quarter

Last Quarter

Eclipse

Sun

FRIDAY	SATURDAY	SUNDAY
		Beltane 1
6	7	8
13	14	15
20	21	22
27	28	29

MAY

goals

MAY

M	T	W	T	F	S	S
25	26	27	28	29	30	1
2	3	4	5	6	7	8
9	10	11	12	13	14	15
16	17	18	19	20	21	22
23	24	25	26	27	28	29
30	31	1	2	3	4	5

LUNAR PHASES

MAY 8TH: FIRST QUARTER IN LEO

Impressing others and receiving praise will give you a sense of safety and sevurity while the moon is in Leo. This only sets you up for failure, as you'll find yourself at a loss as soon as you're put in the spotlight. The key to navigating through Leo is accepting that feedback and criticism are useful, they help you improve. The first step to accepting these facts is to admit you are afraid of criticism, and to admit that you can't accept criticism. Only once you admit the truth of the problem can you work through it.

MAY 16TH: FULL MOON IN SAGITTARIUS (LUNAR ECLIPSE)

The moon in Sagittarius is the most optimistic of energies, giving you a craving for new experiences and adventure. Motivations under the Sagittarius moon are driven by the need for the truth, or finding something, be it a philosophy, a goal or new hobby. You may be inclined to overdo things, so make sure you don't forget to count your blessings and appreciate what you have right now.

MAY 22ND: LAST QUARTER IN AQUARIUS

The moon in Aquarius gives us the need for emotional freedoms which can cause complications in our relationships. Can also be a time when you are able to better understand your emotions, freeing you from negative feelings such as jealousy, fear, and anger.

MAY 30TH: NEW MOON IN GEMINI

Under the Gemini moon you may find that communicating your feelings and emotions becomes easier. Your actions are motivated by the desire for variety and the urge to satisfy curiosity. Just be careful you don't become reckless and fickle – the key is harmony of the mind and heart.

RITUAL PLANNER

GOAL/INTENTION:

ITEMS NEEDED:

STEPS:

MAY HERB PLANTING GUIDE: FAERY GARDENS

The intention behind creating a Faery garden is typically to honor or acknowledge the Fae, to invite them into your life, or a combination of the two. Fae can be powerful magical allies, especially when it comes to gardening. When I planted my first garden I had no clue what I was doing. I knew the basics, but I didn't have the touch. My plants were weak and withering. It was quite heartbreaking to see these plants I had brought to life drom a mere seed struggling for their lives. That's when I decided to reach out to the Good Neighbors (always use euphemisms when you're communicating with the Fae, as calling them faery is offensive). I started turning my pathetic flower and herb garden into a Faery garden.

I purchased fairy statues from the dollar store, made little signs that said things like "Welcome" and "Bright Blessings" that I stuck around the plants of the garden. In the front and middle space of the garden I placed a large, flat stone I found in the woods. With acrylic paint I painted a seven-point star, the faery star, on the rock and glued plastic gems at each point. I announced that I would be sporadically leaving offerings as a sign of respect for the Good Neighbors on the land – never promise to leave offerings on a regular basis unless you're 100% positive you can carry out that promise- and that's just what I did. I usually put a little cup of milk with honey, and sometimes a piece of my morning toast, or a cookie from that evenings' dessert.

There'd be times I'd see something in my home, like an old piece of jewelry or a little knickknack and I'd get the geeling that I should give it to the Fae, so I would. After about a month of this i felt I had gained their trust, so I prepared a really special offering of sweets, milk and honey, handmade gifts, and I brought them out at sunset. I laid them on the stone and turned towards the woods where the clan resided. I greeted them warmly, expressed my gratitude for them letting me live on their land, and finally asked them to help me with the garden.

In exchange I promised to keep planting the garden every spring, and to leave them offerings whenever I thought of it.

That garden went from weed-ridden, drooping and frail to lush with life. Flowers were vivid shades of all colors, many growing taller than me. The weeds that had once threatened to choke the life out of my plants were totally gone 2 weeks later – I never pulled any up, never put down any weed killer, never even used mulch. They just thinned out and stopped growing. I didn't have to water the garden either – it seemed to rain just when the soil started to dry out. I kept the flowers pruned, deadheading, cutting, and such, duties that allowed me to touch each flower, familiarizing myself with its' spirit.

LUCID DREAMING

What is Lucid Dreaming?

Lucid Dreaming is a state in which you realize you are dreaming while currently in a dream. At this point, you can control your entire dream while still asleep without waking up. You can control the scene, individuals, and everything else going on. This enables people to do whatever they like in their dreams as if in a fantasy world. However, many people will realize their dreaming and wake up soon after, not allowing them to continue the lucid dream.

Why, as a Witch, Should I Lucid Dream?

I am a big believer in practical witchcraft. Things that you can do and create instant change. Some experts suggest that mastering lucid dreaming will make astral projection a lot easier to learn. Astral project is an immense skill that many witches aim to learn. It allows you to leave your physical body for a brief time before returning. Lucid dreaming is also essentially creating a fantasy world of anything you like to do, anything you want using the extra hours you usually lose. If that's not magic, what is?

Why, as a Person, Should I Lucid Dream?

Lucid dreaming allows you to work out problems that you may not be able to in waking life. With essentially extra hours being given to you, you can accomplish more. Some have been known to study in their sleep, train, and practice tasks that help them in waking life. More importantly, it is a stress reliever as it is the ultimate "you" time. You can relax, play out a scenario you would typically be unable to, and even just enjoy some quiet time.

Tips to Lucid Dream

When you go to sleep, consciously decide you will lucid dream. This gets the idea into your head, and it will more likely happen.
When starting out, pre-plan what you would like to lucid dream about. You don't want to wake yourself up after becoming lucid because you had to develop a scenario on the spot. As you become more experienced, you won't need to do this.

-Use an app to promote triggers: Apps like "DreamZ" will help train you to lucid dream by sending out a trigger phase once you enter REM sleep. To make the most out of triggers, you even want to use them in waking life to promote the awareness you wish to while dreaming.

-Consider using a Mugwort Tea or Body Oil.

-Make sure you're getting quality rest; turn off lights, tv, and radio as they can make REM sleep more difficult (REM is when lucid dreaming occurs.)

-Stress and being overtired can prevent lucid dreaming, so avoid trying to learn this technique while under a lot of stress. It will take longer to master and will become frustrating.

-GIVE IT TIME! It can take months to successfully accomplish this technique.

-Turn off electronics 30 minutes before bedtime (harder than it seems.)

-Enjoy a melatonin-rich snack before bed (sunflower seeds or cherries would go well with Mugwort tea)

JOURNAL PROMPT

PAUSE & REFLECT

If you could control your dreams, what would you choose to dream about?

MAY FESTIVALS

During the months of April and May, the people of Vanuatu on Pentecost Island perform the Ritual of Naghol, either as a coming-of-age ceremony or to bless the earth for a bountiful yam harvest. The main event of this ritual is land-diving. About 30 men take turns leaping from 75-foot wooden towers. The only thing keeping these men from crashing to their deaths is a vine tied to their ankle. It was this ritual that inspired Bungee Jumping. Dramas and songs are performed before the jump, and the ritual is brough to a close by feasting.
[Source: https://www.mentalfloss.com/article/19055/early-history-bungee-jumping]

USE THE SPACE BELOW TO RECORD YOUR MAY CELEBRATIONS

2 MAY
MONDAY

3 MAY
TUESDAY

6 MAY
FRIDAY

7 MAY
SATURDAY

4 MAY
WEDNESDAY

5 MAY
THURSDAY

8 MAY
SUNDAY

MAY - 2022

	M	T	W	T	F	S	S
17	25	26	27	28	29	30	1
18	2	3	4	5	6	7	8
19	9	10	11	12	13	14	15
20	16	17	18	19	20	21	22
21	23	24	25	26	27	28	29
22	30	31	1	2	3	4	5

9 MAY
MONDAY

10 MAY
TUESDAY

13 MAY
FRIDAY

14 MAY
SATURDAY

11 MAY
WEDNESDAY

12 MAY
THURSDAY

15 MAY
SUNDAY

MAY - 2022

	M	T	W	T	F	S	S
17	25	26	27	28	29	30	1
18	2	3	4	5	6	7	8
19	9	10	11	12	13	14	15
20	16	17	18	19	20	21	22
21	23	24	25	26	27	28	29
22	30	31	1	2	3	4	5

16 MAY
MONDAY

17 MAY
TUESDAY

20 MAY
FRIDAY

21 MAY
SATURDAY

18 MAY
WEDNESDAY

19 MAY
THURSDAY

22 MAY
SUNDAY

MAY - 2022

	M	T	W	T	F	S	S
17	25	26	27	28	29	30	1
18	2	3	4	5	6	7	8
19	9	10	11	12	13	14	15
20	16	17	18	19	20	21	22
21	23	24	25	26	27	28	29
22	30	31	1	2	3	4	5

23 MAY MONDAY

24 MAY TUESDAY

27 MAY FRIDAY

28 MAY SATURDAY

25 MAY WEDNESDAY

26 MAY THURSDAY

29 MAY SUNDAY

MAY - 2022

	M	T	W	T	F	S	S
17	25	26	27	28	29	30	1
18	2	3	4	5	6	7	8
19	9	10	11	12	13	14	15
20	16	17	18	19	20	21	22
21	23	24	25	26	27	28	29
22	30	31	1	2	3	4	5

30 MAY
MONDAY

31 MAY
TUESDAY

3 JUNE
FRIDAY

4 JUNE
SATURDAY

1 JUNE WEDNESDAY

2 JUNE THURSDAY

5 JUNE SUNDAY

JUNE - 2022

	M	T	W	T	F	S	S
22	30	31	1	2	3	4	5
23	6	7	8	9	10	11	12
24	13	14	15	16	17	18	19
25	20	21	22	23	24	25	26
26	27	28	29	30	1	2	3

GRATITUDE LIST

MONTHLY TO-DO'S

TRY SOMETHING NEW

CRYSTALS

Ancient peoples of cultures from all over the world have revered all stones of Jasper as sacred, said to offer protection in the physical and spiritual realms. The red jasper in particular is still used to this day as a stone of protection. The high spiritual energy vibrations allow for an increase in focus and endurance. Red Jasper is a stone of passion, promoting endurance and enhancing the intimacy of love-making, making it a great stone to give to your lover.

CARD SPREAD

Card 1: Who you are- Card 2: What they see - Card 3: How to make it match

SPELL

Spell jars are an excellent, easy, way to work magic. They're versatile, so you can make a jar for just about any intention, whether it's love, creativity, money, protection, and so on. Regardless of what you wish to manifest, you'll need the following: small glass jar, cork stopper, tiny scroll of paper and something to write with. The specifics of the next items will vary, depending on what your intention is. If you wish for more money, then a green candle and a gold ribbon would be perfect, whereas an orange candle and yellow ribbon would be better for creativity.

The same goes for herbs and stones – what you'll need will depend on your intent. I always recommend following your instinct, however. If you are making a jar for love, and feel called to add an onyx stone, then add it, even though it's a stone of protection. It could be your intuition telling you to incorporate a bit of protection, so your love doesn't end up hurting you.

ENTITY

Create honey cakes and fairy wine at dawn for the fae folk.

SELF-CARE

Try a new spell technique that you thought would never be for you.

TEA: Pu Erh Tea

Known as the witch's broom, Pu Erh tea is fermented to create a beloved earthy and smooth tea.

HERBS

Juniper berries, the fruit of the Juniper tree (Juniperus), are great for protection, attraction/lust, love and sex, and make for great offerings to goddesses. String 7 dried berries and hang to protect your work space, steep in vinegar and add to a bath to make yourself more attractive, and have a particularly powerful effect on male virility. Ironically, the berries will abort pregnancy, and therefore should not be used by those who are or may be pregnant.

Record a Card Pull

DECK USED:

CARD(S) PULLED:

YOUR INTERPRETATION:

BOOK INTERPRETATION:

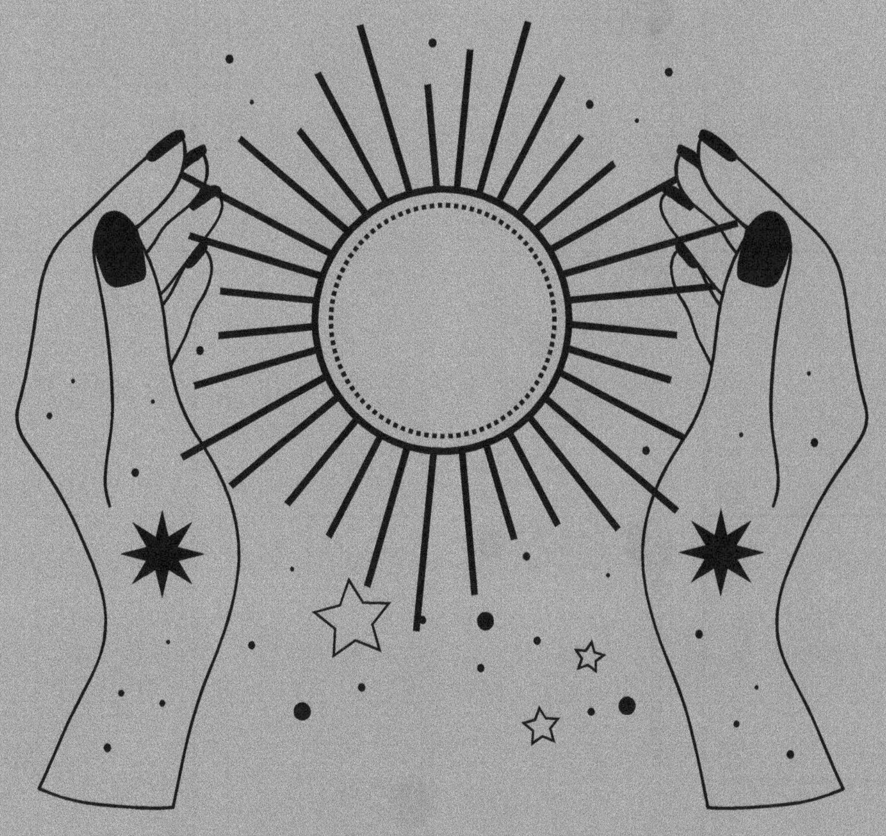

“Healing is a matter of time, but it is sometimes also a matter of opportunity.”

- Hippocrates

MONDAY	TUESDAY	WEDNESDAY	THURSDAY
30	31	1	2
6	[First Quarter] ♍ 7	8	9
13	[Full Moon] ♐ 14	15	16
20	[Last Quarter] ♈ ♋ [Sun] Summer Solstice 21	22	23
27	28	[New Moon] ♋ 29	30

Calendar Key

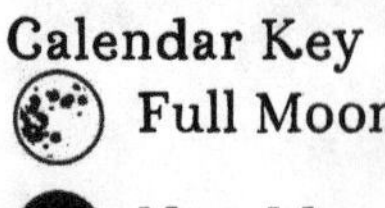

- Full Moon
- New Moon
- First Quarter
- Last Quarter
- Eclipse
- Sun

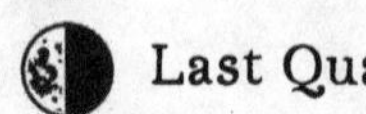

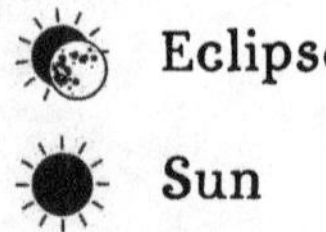

FRIDAY	SATURDAY	SUNDAY
3	4	5
10	11	12
17	18	19
24	25	26

JUN

goals

JUNE

M	T	W	T	F	S	S
30	31	1	2	3	4	5
6	7	8	9	10	11	12
13	14	15	16	17	18	19
20	21	22	23	24	25	26
27	28	29	30	1	2	3

GOALS & DREAMS

6-MONTH PROJECT LIST

GOAL: ______________________________ DUE DATE: __________

ENVISION YOUR LIFE AFTER OBTAINING YOUR GOAL.
HOW DO YOU FEEL?

MONTHLY ACTION STEPS:

NOTES:

LUNAR PHASES

JUNE 7TH: FIRST QUARTER VIRGO

The Virgo moon is one of order and practicality. You feel you have to reorganize and bring order to anything you feel is in chaos. This can lead to being intolerant of others, so try focusing more on solving problems, creating order within your life, and helping others without judgement.

JUNE 14TH: FULL MOON IN SAGITTARIUS

The moon in Sagittarius is the most optimistic of energies, giving you a craving for new experiences and adventure. Motivations under the Sagittarius moon are driven by the need for the truth, or finding something, be it a philosophy, a goal or new hobby. You may be inclined to overdo things, so make sure you don't forget to count your blessings and appreciate what you have right now.

JUNE 21ST: LAST QUARTER IN ARIES

The moon in Aries is emotionally direct and impulsive, with strong, influential feelings. Time for a fresh start, learning new behaviors, establishing new habits. Just don't rush to make decisions, as Aries is apt to do, feeling as though quicker is better. It's not. Take your time to consider what you need, what you want, and choose carefully. The choices made in Aries set the tone for the extended future.

JUNE 29TH: NEW MOON IN CANCER

The Moon in Cancer instills in you emotional security and a sense of belonging, a sense of nurturing you feel instinctively. You find that you're longing for an intimate connection that's meaningful and long-lasting, enough so you can establish a sense of belonging-put down roots, a place to bunker down as the Universe throws its' trials and tribulations at you. Using the Full Moon energies to work a self-love spell may help to satisfy this desire.

RITUAL PLANNER

GOAL/INTENTION:

ITEMS NEEDED:

STEPS:

JUNE HERB GUIDE

Bees and Butterflies are environmentally vital, beneficial to our gardens, and make excellent magical allies. Bees are amazing communicators, highly productive, possess incredible endurance and determination, and are natures collectors. Channeling the Bee can aid you in the collection of wisdom, instill endurance and determination in the pursuit of your goals, and help you learn to communicate clearly and effectively. Butterflies are symbols of transformation, and can even aid in spiritual shapeshifting, as they transition from a worm-like caterpillar to the delicate, beautiful butterfly.

ERB	SIZE/ SPREAD	START SEEDS INSIDE/OUTSIDE	HARDINESS ZONE	NATIVE REGION	GROWTH TYPE**	SUN/- SOIL**
nise ssop	2-4'/1.5-3'	Direct Sow in Fall	4-9	Europe, North Africa, some parts of Asia	A	FS/WD
ill	2-4'/2-3'	10-12/ NR – seed needs soil	9-11	Peru	P	FS/RL
nnel	4-6'/18-36"	8-12/ 1-2 before	5-8	Mediterranean Region	P	FS/WD
nmer vory	12-18"/3'	NR/ after frost	4-9	North America	P	FS/M,WD

eeks before or afer last spring frost

=Annual P=Perennial

S= full sun, PS= partial sun; WD= well-drained, M= moist, RM, rich moint, L= loamy, LS=loamy/sandy

Magic Properties:
Anise Hyssop: Protection, Purification, Cleansing, Blessings
Dill: Love Spells, Dispel Bad Dreams and Jealousy, Emotional Balance
Fennel: Courage, Strength, Protection, Love/Fertility, Divination
Summer Savory: Enhance Sex Life ,Improve Concentration and Memory, Empowerment

Record a Card Pull

DECK USED:

CARD(S) PULLED:

YOUR INTERPRETATION:

BOOK INTERPRETATION:

MEDITATION ON THE MOVE

Moving meditation is a game-changer, witches. I have ADD, so establishing a meditation practice has been painful. It was until I learned about moving meditation. Now, I get my 20 minutes of meditation every day, and I don't have to force myself to sit still. In fact, I've even lost weight because I've been more active!

What it Means to Meditate

What is meditation, exactly? Most people think that meditation is to sit quietly and clear their minds. They worry so much about not thinking. All they can do is think. But that's not what meditation is all about. Meditating helps you slow down your thoughts, allowing you to not only understand what you're thinking but why. Diana Rajchel, of "13 Meditations for a Short Attention Span" (Llewellyns' 2014 Magical Almanac), states that the one rule of meditation is that you are turning communication inward, explaining that meditation consists of "going within, observing, and engaging wholly with yourself...". (p.106). So this means that meditation does not have to be done sitting perfectly still in a darkened room – as long as you can focus on the wanderings of your mind, you can meditate.

Moving Meditation

What does moving meditation look like? It can look like any activity you can do that allows you to move and turn communication inward. My favorite form of moving meditation is painting. When my son is asleep, the house is quiet. I set up a canvas and lay down my brushes. I take a breath, sketch the image in my mind, and I just dive into the painting. It's soothing, laying down the underpainting, adding detail, gradually building the picture. The sound of the brush is rhythmic, lulling, and my mind quiets. Just see what works for you. This will be a process of trial and error- don't stress if you don't find a suitable activity right away. What counts is that you keep trying. Doing something that has a rhythm to it tends to work best. This can be walking, biking, washing dishes, sewing by hand, painting, climbing a set of stairs- find your rhythm, and you've found mediation in motion.

PAUSE & REFLECT

What is your personal magical philosophy?

JUNE FESTIVALS

June is known as Pride Month in the United States. Three important events in the gay liberation movement took place in June. The first being the Stonewall Riots on June 29th, 1969, which was a series of demonstrations by the LGBTQIA+ community and their supporters in response to the police raids on the Stonewall Inn in Greenwich Village, NY on June 28th.
June 28th, 1970 marks the date of the first gay pride marches which were carried out simultaneously in New York, Los Angeles, and San Francisco.
On June 26, 2015, the U.S. Supreme Court struck down all state bans on same-sex marriage, legalized it in all fifty states.

[Source: https://youth.gov/feature-article/june-lgbt-pride-month]

USE THE SPACE BELOW TO RECORD YOUR JUNE CELEBRATIONS

6 JUNE
MONDAY

7 JUNE
TUESDAY

10 JUNE
FRIDAY

11 JUNE
SATURDAY

8 JUNE
WEDNESDAY

9 JUNE
THURSDAY

12 JUNE
SUNDAY

JUNE - 2022

	M	T	W	T	F	S	S
22	30	31	1	2	3	4	5
23	6	7	8	9	10	11	12
24	13	14	15	16	17	18	19
25	20	21	22	23	24	25	26
26	27	28	29	30	1	2	3

13 JUNE
MONDAY

14 JUNE
TUESDAY

17 JUNE
FRIDAY

18 JUNE
SATURDAY

15 JUNE WEDNESDAY

16 JUNE THURSDAY

19 JUNE SUNDAY

JUNE - 2022

	M	T	W	T	F	S	S
22	30	31	1	2	3	4	5
23	6	7	8	9	10	11	12
24	13	14	15	16	17	18	19
25	20	21	22	23	24	25	26
26	27	28	29	30	1	2	3

20 JUNE
MONDAY

21 JUNE
TUESDAY

24 JUNE
FRIDAY

25 JUNE
SATURDAY

22 JUNE WEDNESDAY

23 JUNE THURSDAY

26 JUNE SUNDAY

JUNE - 2022

	M	T	W	T	F	S	S
22	30	31	1	2	3	4	5
23	6	7	8	9	10	11	12
24	13	14	15	16	17	18	19
25	20	21	22	23	24	25	26
26	27	28	29	30	1	2	3

27 JUNE MONDAY

28 JUNE TUESDAY

1 JULY FRIDAY

2 JULY SATURDAY

29 JUNE
WEDNESDAY

30 JUNE
THURSDAY

3 JULY
SUNDAY

JUNE - 2022

	M	T	W	T	F	S	S
22	30	31	1	2	3	4	5
23	6	7	8	9	10	11	12
24	13	14	15	16	17	18	19
25	20	21	22	23	24	25	26
26	27	28	29	30	1	2	3

GRATITUDE LIST

MONTHLY TO-DO'S

TRY SOMETHING NEW

CRYSTALS

When you first acquire a crystal, and before using crystals in rituals or spells, they should be cleansed. This means you need to clear the energies that have 'stuck' to the stone over time. There are many ways to cleanse crystals, and the method depends on the type of crystal. For example, leaving crystals in the sun will cleanse them, but some crystals, like amethyst, will fade in the sun and therefore should not be cleansed like this. Water is another way to cleanse energies, either by holding the stone under running water, or soaking the stone in salt water. This method is not recommended for all crystals, as some may be broken down by the water, while others may have a toxic reaction to the water. Using the light of the full moon, and energetic cleansing, (when you envision white light descending from above and filling the stones, cleansing their

CARD SPREAD

Card 1: Book to read - Card 2: Movie to watch - Card 3: Music to listen to

SPELL

Healing Blemishes: This spell has been passed down for generations on my grandmother's side of the family. The origins are unknown, but anyone of Acadian/French Canadian descent will likely recognize this little working. If you have a blemish, be it a wart or a mole or a pimple, cut a potato in half and rub it on the blemish. Then take the potato outside and bury it. If you wish you can say an incantation, such as: "As this potato rots in the ground my blemish will fade away until no trace is found".

ENTITY

When working on a ritual, think of a passed ancestor you believe may have been a witch and invite them to join your working.

SELF-CARE

Clean out your voicemails - just do it, it'll make a difference.

TEA: Earl Grey Lavender Tea

Earl grey is a beloved tea that features a crisp bergamot flavor. Paired with a few lavender leaves this tea is bright, floral, and perfect for the summer

HERBS

A decoction is a form of infusion of herbs. Add the roots, stem, and/or bark, to a pan of cold water (a quarter ounce of dried herbs per cup of water) and bring to a boil. Cover and let simmer for 15-20 minutes. Take off the heat, and leave it covered for about 20 minutes. Strain and store in a jar in a cool, dry place. A decoction of pine, mint, and lime peel makes an excellent cleaning potion.

Record a Card Pull

DECK USED:

CARD(S) PULLED:

YOUR INTERPRETATION:

BOOK INTERPRETATION:

"Everything, absolutely everything on this earth makes sense, and even the smallest things are worthy of our consideration."

-Paulo Coelho, The Witch of Portobello

MONDAY	TUESDAY	WEDNESDAY	THURSDAY
27	28	29	30
4	5	First Quarter ♎ 6	7
11	12	Full Moon ♑ 13	14
18	19	Last Quarter ♈ 20	21
25	26	27	New Moon ♌ 28

Calendar Key

Full Moon

New Moon

 First Quarter

 Last Quarter

 Eclipse

 Sun

FRIDAY	SATURDAY	SUNDAY
1	2	3
8	9	10
15	16	17
22	☉♌ 23	24
29	30	31

JUL

goals

JULY

M	T	W	T	F	S	S
27	28	29	30	1	2	3
4	5	6	7	8	9	10
11	12	13	14	15	16	17
18	19	20	21	22	23	24
25	26	27	28	29	30	31

LUNAR PHASES

JULY 6TH: FIRST QUARTER IN LIBRA

The moon in Libra drives us for a sense of order, but unlike that of the moon in Virgo, we are satisfied by pleasant interactions and aesthetics in the environment. The need for order and harmony are strong, and rather than deal with confrontation you try to keep everything 'nice'. Don't let the Libra moon make you forget who you are, and certainly resist the urge to bottle up your feelings.

JULY 13TH: FULL MOON IN CAPRICORN

The moon in Capricorn has an emotional seriousness, a sober orientation, and a practical awareness that brings with it a need to feel useful. Using the energies of the new moon and amplified ambitions of Capricorn, this is an ideal time to start new projects.

JULY 20TH: LAST QUARTER IN ARIES

The moon in Aries is emotionally direct and impulsive, with strong, influential feelings. Time for a fresh start, learning new behaviors, establishing new habits. Just don't rush to make decisions, as Aries is apt to do, feeling as though quicker is better. It's not. Take your time to consider what you need, what you want, and choose carefully. The choices made in Aries set the tone for the extended future.

JULY 28TH: NEW MOON IN LEO

Impressing others and receiving praise will give you a sense of safety and sevurity while the moon is in Leo. This only sets you up for failure, as you'll find yourself at a loss as soon as you're put in the spotlight. The key to navigating through Leo is accepting that feedback and criticism are useful, they help you improve. The first step to accepting these facts is to admit you are afraid of criticism, and to admit that you can't accept criticism. Only once you admit the truth of the problem can you work through it.

RITUAL PLANNER

GOAL/INTENTION:

ITEMS NEEDED:

STEPS:

JULY FESTIVALS

The Festival of San Fermin, locally known as Sanfermines, is a week-long festival celebrated in Spain to honor the first Spanish bishop, Saint Fermin. While the festival is best known for the Running of the Bulls, there are a number of other traditional and folkloric events that take place at the Festival of San Fermin. The festival commences by setting off a firework, the "chupinazo", a rocket launched at noon on July 6th from a city hall balcony while thousands of people celebrate in the city hall square.

July 7th features the Saint Fermin procession, an event in which thousands of people accompany the 15th century statue of Saint Fermin through the old section of Pamplona. The procession is joined by street performers, dancers, and the emergence of 'gigantes', gigantic wood-framed-paper-mâché puppets controlled from the inside, which dance and twirl down the street when the cathedral bell "Maria" starts to ring. The festival ends at midnight of July 14th, with everyone gathered in the candle-lit city square singing Pobre de mí.

[Source: https://en.wikipedia.org/wiki/Festival_of_San_Ferm%C3%ADn]

JULY HERBAL PLANTING GUIDE: GARDENING METHODS

Once you decide on what you want to plant, you'll have to decide how you'll plant them – the gardening method. The most common gardening methods are in-ground, raised row, raised bed, and container, and there are benefits and drawbacks to each method.

In-Ground Gardening

In-ground gardens are just as they sound- you'll dig up the grass, pull out rocks and weeds, add nutrient rich soil and plant directly into the ground. While this is the most affordable method of gardening, it requires the most time and effort to create and maintain.

Raised Row Gardening

Raised Row gardens are in-ground gardens with raised areas of soil and organic material (i.e. compost, shredded leaves, mulch, straw) formed into rows or hills. The goal of a raised row garden is to build mounds of rich, healthy soil that continually breaks down, improving the entire garden space. Building the mounds will take some time and effort, and high quality soil can be fairly expensive, but maintenance of the garden is minimal because you won't have to weed and pests are less likely to be an issue, and you'll have a higher yield and longer growing time because the higher mounds allow for a deeper, stronger root system.

Raised Bed Gardening

A raised garden bed is a bottomless container, made of either wood, plastic, stone, or concrete, filled with high-quality soil that sits on top of the ground. The raised bed could be purchased, custom built, or you could build it yourself. Pick a sunny part of your lawn to put the bed and fill it about a quarter of the way with organic matter (i.e. compost), then fill it up to about 2" below the top of the frame with mid to high-quality soil. As the organic matter breaks down it will enhance the soil, and allowing for deep and strong root systems which will prevent weed growth. To deter pests either cover the bed with a screen or tent or plant pest-deterring plants.

Container Gardening

A container garden is one that grows in a container. If the container can hold soil, then you can use it to hold a garden- so long as you can drill holes in the bottom to allow for drainage (not applicable to grow bags because they are not watertight). Some possible containers you could use are traditional pots, boxes, bins, grow bags, barrels, troughs, tubs - even a tin can. This method is ideal for people who don't have a yard or space to put down a garden, are unable or don't wish to spend a great deal of time outside or participating in a physically exerting activity.

One of the major benefits to this method is that you have control over the growing conditions. This method could be expensive but there are ways to cut costs without depriving the plants, such as using a container you have in your home instead of buying a new plant pot.

WATER MAGIC

Water is the element of emotion, as it is unpredictable, flowing, and strong. Water is a great tool for cleansing, clearing, expelling, and expanding. I have three Water magic activities for you to try this month. The first uses water and air to make a wish. The second brings you to an ocean -either in person or in the astral, to connect with the spirits of the Sea. The third is a ritual bath, to keep you cool, calm, and collected when the summer heat combines with the pressures at work, home, and/or internally.

Bubble Wish

We all have wishes – longer hair, slimmer waist, fatter wallet, faster car. Whatever the wish, we have the power to make it happen. We are connected and in tune to the Universe, and know that what we believe on the inside, the universe will send to us on the outside. Go to your local dollar store and get a little bottle of bubbles. You'll want to keep it with your magical supplies, so if you have kids you should get two, as any kid who sees you blowing bubbles will want to blow some of their own. If you wish, take the bottle to your altar or sacred space to cleanse it energetically. Take the bottle outside, open the cap and think about your wish. See it in your mind clearly. Imagine how you'll feel, what you'll see, smell, hear- bring that wish true in your mind. When you're ready, load the little wand with bubble mixture and hold it up in front of your mouth. Speak your wish and say thank you. Then take a deep breath and blow gently, letting the bubbles grow and break free from the wand and blow away with the breeze. Take a moment to be mindful of the land around you, the sky above, and the life all around. Tell the universe thank you one more time and put your bubbles away with your other magical supplies.

Spirits of the Sea

Spirits of the sea are powerful magical allies who are excellent at helping us achieve goals, heal our bodies and mind, and understanding and regulating our emotions. Before you reach out to the sea spirits, create an altar in honor of the sea. Use colors of blue, green, and beige. Place bowls or jars salt water and sand on the altar and decorate it with seashells and representations of starfish and sand dollars. Pin photos of oceans and islands on the wall behind it. Each day stand before the altar and call to the element of water, feeling the energy of the sea manifesting. When the altar feels ready, and worthy of honoring a sea spirit, go to the ocean. If you don't live by an ocean, get into a meditative state and imagine yourself standing before the ocean. Stand (or imagine you're standing) where the water meets the sand, as this is a liminal space and therefore most magical. If you wish to contact a particular sea spirit, you may do so, or you can address the spirits in general. Tell them who you are and that you would like to make a connection with them. I wouldn't start off by asking for favors - working with spirits is like working with people. You wouldn't start a friendship off by asking someone to help you move your tv or to wash your car, so don't start a connection with a spirit with a favor. Let them know that you have a place in your home where they can come and communicate with you.

You may wish to ask for an omen, such as seeing a seabird flying to or from the west. Be patient, gently sending your thoughts back to the ocean now and then until you are contacted. Take your time building a relationship and establishing trust. It may take two weeks, or it might take two months. But when you reach a point where you can turn to the spirit for magical assistance you'll see that it was well worth the time and effort.

Calm, Cool, and Collected Ritual Bath (Shower)

For this bath you'll need a cucumber, peeled, and sliced, Eucalyptus oil, and Grapeseed carrier oil. You'll mix the Eucalyptus oil with a carrier oil, like Almond or Avocado oil (12 drops per fluid ounce of oil). You can pour a cup of the mixed oil into the tub as it fills or rub it on your skin before taking a shower. Add the slices of cucumber to the tub (or take a couple into the shower to place over your eyes). The water should be cool or lukewarm (just not so cold you shiver or get goosebumps).

When you're in the water, close your eyes and take deep, slow breaths. Visualize yourself swimming in a glacial pool, or standing under a glacial waterfall. As the water and cooling oils seep into your body, absorb the refreshing magic they possess. You are feeling calm, cool, and refreshed. The coolness will clear your mind, expel stress and anxiety, and give you the energy you'll need to face things you must, and forget things that aren't worthy of your worry. Say aloud or think to yourself: No matter the heat I face, I remain calm, cool, and collected.

This bath/shower can be done anytime. When you feel yourself overwhelmed at work or with your kids (or anywhere, really), take a moment for yourself. Bring to mind the scent of the eucalyptus, the refreshing properties of the cucumbers, and breathe through the stress. Repeat the affirmation as often as you need.

Magic of Water

Water is an incredible part of this world. It creates and sustains life; it cleans and purifies; it conducts energy, making it an excellent tool for magic. The peak of summer is the hottest, but thanks to water, you'll remain cool.

PAUSE & REFLECT

How did you develop your altar? Why is it set up the way that it is?

4 JULY
MONDAY

5 JULY
TUESDAY

8 JULY
FRIDAY

9 JULY
SATURDAY

6 JULY
WEDNESDAY

7 JULY
THURSDAY

10 JULY
SUNDAY

JULY - 2022

	M	T	W	T	F	S	S
26	27	28	29	30	1	2	3
27	4	5	6	7	8	9	10
28	11	12	13	14	15	16	17
29	18	19	20	21	22	23	24
30	25	26	27	28	29	30	31

11 JULY
MONDAY

12 JULY
TUESDAY

15 JULY
FRIDAY

16 JULY
SATURDAY

13 JULY WEDNESDAY

14 JULY THURSDAY

17 JULY SUNDAY

JULY - 2022

	M	T	W	T	F	S	S
26	27	28	29	30	1	2	3
27	4	5	6	7	8	9	10
28	11	12	13	14	15	16	17
29	18	19	20	21	22	23	24
30	25	26	27	28	29	30	31

18 JULY MONDAY

19 JULY TUESDAY

22 JULY FRIDAY

23 JULY SATURDAY

20 JULY WEDNESDAY

21 JULY THURSDAY

24 JULY SUNDAY

JULY - 2022

	M	T	W	T	F	S	S
26	27	28	29	30	1	2	3
27	4	5	6	7	8	9	10
28	11	12	13	14	15	16	17
29	18	19	20	21	22	23	24
30	25	26	27	28	29	30	31

25 JULY
MONDAY

26 JULY
TUESDAY

29 JULY
FRIDAY

30 JULY
SATURDAY

27 JULY WEDNESDAY

28 JULY THURSDAY

31 JULY SUNDAY

JULY - 2022

	M	T	W	T	F	S	S
26	27	28	29	30	1	2	3
27	4	5	6	7	8	9	10
28	11	12	13	14	15	16	17
29	18	19	20	21	22	23	24
30	25	26	27	28	29	30	31

GRATITUDE LIST

MONTHLY TO-DO'S

TRY SOMETHING NEW

CRYSTALS

Hematite is the ultimate protector stone. This black stone does have magnetic properties and should not be used by those with a pace maker. Hematite absorbs negative energies and calms stress, and has excellent balancing qualities, so if you're having a rough day just carry a piece of hematite around in your pocket.

Use hematite beads to make protective amulets for the home or car. Add to sachets for protection, or put on your altar to keep your energies clear, calm, and balanced.

Source: https://www.healingcrystals.com/Hematite_Articles_101.html

CARD SPREAD

Card 1: The Conflict - Card 2: The Obstacle - Card 3: The Solution

SPELL

Courage Spell: This spell is inspired by the Eye of the Tiger Courage Spell by Storm Faerywolf, found in Llewellyn's 2021 Witches' Spell-A-Day Almanac.

Get a piece of tigers eye and anoint it with either cinnamon oil or dragons blood oil – they are both great for adding a boost to magical workings. Hold the gem in your power hand and say "With the tiger by my side, I need not run, I need not hide. I have courage of the tiger, and I roar with pride."

ENTITY

Meditate to connect to a crossed over spirit and communicate with them to obtain any needed messages.

SELF-CARE

Eat cake today. Screw society. Use your hands. I won't judge.

TEA

Matcha Tea - If you were to take green tea and powder it, you would get matcha. When stirred into hot water it creates a bright green magical potion. It is delicious with steamed milk and helps with focus and energy.

HERBS

Ginger root, or ginger, (Zingiber officinale) grows all over Asia, is vastly popular for its crisp, spicy flavor. Powdered ginger root is a feisty addition to spells to increase the magic or give a boost to personal power. Ginger is a great option for sex magic and spells involving luck, prosperity, healing, protection, and retribution.

Record a Card Pull

DECK USED:

CARD(S) PULLED:

YOUR INTERPRETATION:

BOOK INTERPRETATION:

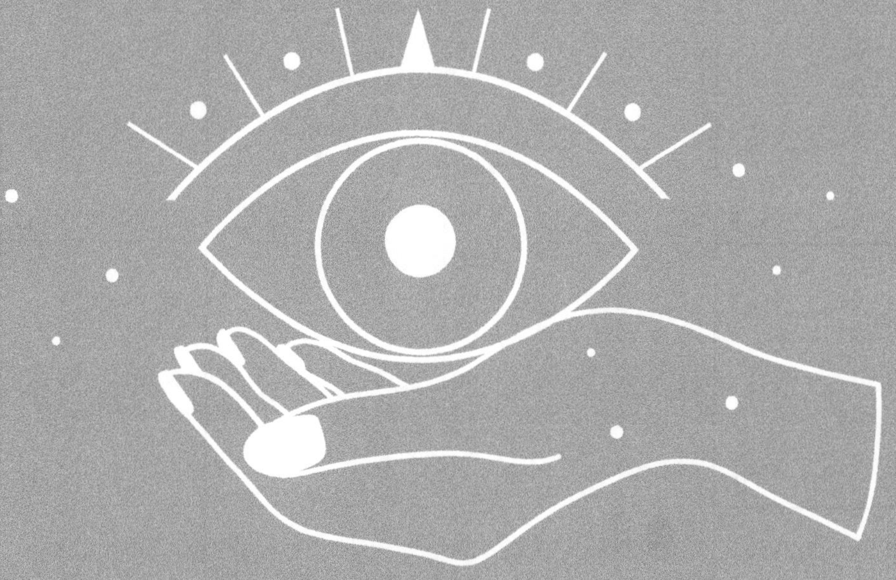

How do you know I'm not making it up? You don't. Things work because you believe in them. Call it faith or will or coincidence or whatever. If you believe it will help to light a candle and ask the universe to help you understand the mystery and meaning of the Hierophant, then it will. Don't spend a bunch of money on learning how to get to know your cards. Just do it. Say hi to them and get to work."

-Melissa Cynova

MONDAY	TUESDAY	WEDNESDAY	THURSDAY
Lammas 1	2	3	4
8	9	10	11
15	16	17	18
22	☉♍ 23	24	25
29	30	31	

Calendar Key

Full Moon

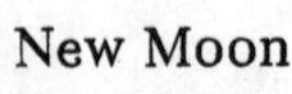
New Moon

First Quarter

Last Quarter

Eclipse

Sun

FRIDAY	SATURDAY	SUNDAY
5	6	7
12	13	14
19	20	21
26	27	28

AUG

goals

AUGUST

M	T	W	T	F	S	S
1	2	3	4	5	6	7
8	9	10	11	12	13	14
15	16	17	18	19	20	21
22	23	24	25	26	27	28
29	30	31	1	2	3	4

LUNAR PHASES

AUGUST 5TH: FIRST QUARTER IN SCORPIO

Scorpio energy encourages us to explore our feelings more deeply, and we find we're drawn to sex, power and money. Learning what gets other people going is arousing. Instinctive orientation is to start over from scratch. Only by destroying the roots of disturbances can you begin healing.

AUGUST 12TH: FULL MOON IN AQUARIUS

The moon in Aquarius gives us the need for emotional freedoms which can cause complications in our relationships. Can also be a time when you are able to better understand your emotions, freeing you from negative feelings such as jealousy, fear, and anger.

AUGUST 19TH: LAST QUARTER IN TAURUS

Your sense of safety arises from the need for stability which is difficult to find at the moment. The key to stability is acceptance - accepting that change is a part of life, and acceptance of who you are as a person. When you accept yourself you will find that peace and tranquility are much easier to come by in your daily life.

AUGUST 27TH: NEW MOON IN VIRGO

The Virgo moon is one of order and practicality. You feel you have to reorganize and bring order to anything you feel is in chaos. This can lead to being intolerant of others, so try focusing more on solving problems, creating order within your life, and helping others without judgement.

RITUAL PLANNER

GOAL/INTENTION:

ITEMS NEEDED:

STEPS:

AUGUST HERBS

Growing the herbs listed above in a window garden would serve any kitchen witch well as they offer a number of magical properties. Whether you need to work magic for health or wealth, for protection or strength, to aid with spirit work or get in touch with the Divine- even if you want to work a glamour or weight loss spell, you'll be covered.

You'll need air-tight containers to store the herbs once you harvest and dry them. Mason jars are excellent for this purpose. I recommend purchasing a sheet of jar labels as well, recording the kind of herb and the date they were dried. Herbs dried and stored in air-tight containers will retain their flavor for up to a year.

You may wish to get a mortar and pestle reserved solely for magical purposes, as it can become charged with your magic, amplifying the power of the herbs ground within it (that's how it seems to work for me anyways).

HERB	SIZE/ SPREAD	START SEEDS INSIDE/OUTSIDE	HARDINESS ZONE	NATIVE REGION	GROWTH TYPE**	SUN/ SOIL*
Thyme	2-12"/7-12"	6-10/2-3	5-9	Paleartic regions of Europe and Asia	P	FS/WD
Oregano	12-24"/18"	6-10	5-12	Mediterranean region of West Asia	P	FS/WD
Parsley	18-24"/6-8"	10-12/3-4 After	4-9	Mediterranean regions of South Eruope and West Asia	B	PS/R
Chives	12-18"	8-10/3-4	3-12	Temperate areas of Europe, Asia and North America	P	FS/RM

*Weeks before or afer last spring frost

** A=Annual P=Perennial

** FS= full sun, PS= partial sun; WD= well-drained, M= moist, RM, rich moint, L= loamy, LS=loamy/sandy

Magic Properties:
Thyme: Good Health, Loyalty, Affection, Strength, Courage, Improve Finances
Oregano: Joy, Strength, Vitality and Added Energy
Parsley: Death, Rebirth, Connecting with Higher Self
Chives: Protection, Weight Loss

ASTRAL SACRED SPACE

August is such an anxiety-riddled time for me. The summer is coming to an end, so all the summer goals I've yet to meet are looming over my head. Creeping up behind me is Fall, which means holidays, school starting, preparing for winter. I'm sure it's not much different for you. With all this stuff going on, you probably wish you had a place to hide out to unwind. A sacred space just for you. Well, I can help you build such a place, all you need is somewhere to sit and maybe a timer.

Building your astral hide-away is a process, but I think it's part of the fun. The only trick is finding the time. If you have to, go to your astral home while you're sitting on the toilet. Who cares if your family thinks you're taking a big poop if it means you have a place to just chill and forget everything bugging you? Just close your eyes, steady your breathing, and feel yourself lift up and away. When your spirit settles in the perfect place, be in a deserted island or the moon, you can start building.

You could build a hut, a house, a mansion if that's what you want. See the foundation, the skeleton of the building, then the walls and then the roof. Walk inside, and as soon as you imagine what you want, it will appear. You may want to set a timer for your astral adventures. You may feel you've only been there a few minutes to find you have been away for almost an hour.

Every day spend at least five minutes in your astral hide-away. When you're there, kick back and relax. Play a game. Go for a swim with mermaids or fly on your pet dragon. It doesn't matter what you do, because the very act of taking time outside of yourself is therapeutic. When you return, take a few minutes to firmly ground yourself. Drink something, eat something, say "I'm home" out loud if you need to. You'll find that you feel refreshed, invigorated, and ready to take on whatever life has to throw at you.

PAUSE & REFLECT

Do you need to update your routine? If so, do it here!

AUGUST FESTIVALS

August 1st is marked as the Celtic holiday Lughnasadh. This holiday was originally celebrated in Ireland, Scotland, and the Isle of Man to mark the beginning of the harvest season. Festivities consisted of competitions and feasts, celebrating love and appreciation for the land, for kin, and for spirits. According to Irish mythology, the very first Lughnasadh was organized by the god Lugh himself in honor of his foster mother, Tailtiu. Tailtiu cleared the way for the introduction of agriculture in Ireland, so there would be no harvest if it weren't for her.
[Source: https://druidry.org/druid-way/teaching-and-practice/druid-festivals/lughnasadh]

USE THE SPACE BELOW TO RECORD YOUR AUGUST CELEBRATIONS

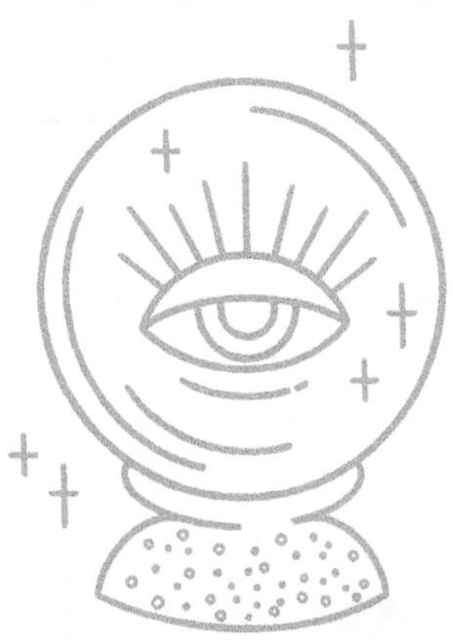

1 AUGUST MONDAY

2 AUGUST TUESDAY

5 AUGUST FRIDAY

6 AUGUST SATURDAY

3 AUGUST
WEDNESDAY

4 AUGUST
THURSDAY

7 AUGUST
SUNDAY

AUGUST - 2022

	M	T	W	T	F	S	S
31	1	2	3	4	5	6	7
32	8	9	10	11	12	13	14
33	15	16	17	18	19	20	21
34	22	23	24	25	26	27	28
35	29	30	31	1	2	3	4

8 AUGUST
MONDAY

9 AUGUST
TUESDAY

12 AUGUST
FRIDAY

13 AUGUST
SATURDAY

10 AUGUST
WEDNESDAY

11 AUGUST
THURSDAY

14 AUGUST
SUNDAY

AUGUST - 2022

	M	T	W	T	F	S	S
31	1	2	3	4	5	6	7
32	8	9	10	11	12	13	14
33	15	16	17	18	19	20	21
34	22	23	24	25	26	27	28
35	29	30	31	1	2	3	4

15 AUGUST
MONDAY

16 AUGUST
TUESDAY

19 AUGUST
FRIDAY

20 AUGUST
SATURDAY

17 AUGUST
WEDNESDAY

18 AUGUST
THURSDAY

21 AUGUST
SUNDAY

AUGUST - 2022

	M	T	W	T	F	S	S
31	1	2	3	4	5	6	7
32	8	9	10	11	12	13	14
33	15	16	17	18	19	20	21
34	22	23	24	25	26	27	28
35	29	30	31	1	2	3	4

22 AUGUST
MONDAY

23 AUGUST
TUESDAY

26 AUGUST
FRIDAY

27 AUGUST
SATURDAY

24 AUGUST
WEDNESDAY

25 AUGUST
THURSDAY

28 AUGUST
SUNDAY

AUGUST - 2022

	M	T	W	T	F	S	S
31	1	2	3	4	5	6	7
32	8	9	10	11	12	13	14
33	15	16	17	18	19	20	21
34	22	23	24	25	26	27	28
35	29	30	31	1	2	3	4

29 AUGUST
MONDAY

30 AUGUST
TUESDAY

2 SEPTEMBER
FRIDAY

3 SEPTEMBER
SATURDAY

31 AUGUST
WEDNESDAY

1 SEPTEMBER
THURSDAY

4 SEPTEMBER
SUNDAY

SEPTEMBER - 2022

	M	T	W	T	F	S	S
35	29	30	31	1	2	3	4
36	5	6	7	8	9	10	11
37	12	13	14	15	16	17	18
38	19	20	21	22	23	24	25
39	26	27	28	29	30	1	2

GRATITUDE LIST

MONTHLY TO-DO'S

TRY SOMETHING NEW

CRYSTALS

Once you have cleansed your crystal you must charge it with your intention. To charge a crystal, hold it in your hand, or set it on your altar or tabletop and hold your power hand over it. Envision your intention, and let the energy of your desire fill your body. When you feel your body brimming with the energy of your visions, send that energy down your arm and out of your palm, straight into the crystal. Once you see (psychically) the stone fill with the energy, ground and center your personal energies. When you touch or hold the crystal, you may see or feel the energy it now holds. Many times I've had crystals vibrating slightly once charged, feeling the subtle buzz of the energy when I touch or hold the crystal.

CARD SPREAD

1: Magic to cast - Card 2: Magic to avoid - Card 3: Magic to monitor

SPELL

Spell to Request Faery Protection and Care for your Garden: Gardens are amazing, and anyone who has nurtured a plant from seed to flower knows how much love you develop for the little plants under your care. I was not born with a green thumb, and until I wrote and worked this spell, my garden was nothing more than a plant graveyard. When you prepare your garden in the spring, and plant all of your little seedlings or seeds, get some dried chamomile, an offering – something sweet or shiny – and head out to your garden. Sprinkle the chamomile around and over the garden, slowly and evenly. Then set the offering in the middle of the garden – if you wish you can set an offering stone down in the middle, so you have a flat sturdy surface. Once you're done, you'll invite the Faeries (but don't call them faeires, say Good Neighbors, Mother's Blessings, or some other Euphemism you feel will honor them). Close your eyes and call the Good Neighbors to your side. When you feel them near, tell them that you have laid an offering of (whatever it is you chose- I usually go with shiny costume jewelry and a cookie or milk with honey), and request that in exchange for the offering they help you care for and protect the garden. Acknowledge that this land was theirs first, so no one but they knows the land so well. Tell them you would very much appreciate the help but don't say "thank you". If you think you can keep the promise, you may offer to leave one offering a week. I have a terrible memory, and ADD, so I say, "I'll give offerings throughout the summer, sporadically, to express my respect and gratitude". Wait a few moments to see if they send you any messages psychically, and when the time is right, bid the Good Neighbors farewell, and do your best to remember to leave offerings as you promised.

ENTITY

Meditate to connect with a spirit of place and try to gain information about your home and space.

SELF-CARE

Stay up an extra hour or two tonight and watch that show you love. It's worth it.

TEA

Soothing Tea - Blend rooibos, orange peels, hibiscus, and lavender to create a tea that is ideal for warm summer days out within nature.

HERBS

Cayenne Pepper is a spicy herb found in the bravest of kitchens. Keep milk on hand when handling this spicy powder, as the milk will neutralize the capsaicin. This fiery herb is great for spells involving protection, banishment, or curses to drive away your enemies.

Record a Card Pull

DECK USED:

CARD(S) PULLED:

YOUR INTERPRETATION:

BOOK INTERPRETATION:

"Witches listen to the secrets of the Earth, work in harmony with the powers of the moon and understand the longings of the human soul."

-Dacha Avelin

MONDAY	TUESDAY	WEDNESDAY	THURSDAY
29	30	31	1
5	6	7	8
12	13	14	15
19	20	21	Fall Equinox/Mabon 22
26	27	28	29

Calendar Key

Full Moon

 First Quarter

 Eclipse

New Moon

 Last Quarter

 Sun

SEP

FRIDAY	SATURDAY	SUNDAY
2	3	4
9	10	11
16	17	18
23	24	25
30		

goals

SEPTEMBER

M	T	W	T	F	S	S
29	30	31	1	2	3	4
5	6	7	8	9	10	11
12	13	14	15	16	17	18
19	20	21	22	23	24	25
26	27	28	29	30	1	2

LUNAR PHASES

SEPTEMBER 3RD: FIRST QUARTER IN SAGITTARIUS

The moon in Sagittarius is the most optimistic of energies, giving you a craving for new experiences and adventure. Motivations under the Sagittarius moon are driven by the need for the truth, or finding something, be it a philosophy, a goal or new hobby. You may be inclined to overdo things, so make sure you don't forget to count your blessings and appreciate what you have right now.

SEPTEMBER 10TH: FULL MOON IN PISCES

The moon in Pisces is a great time for a creative or spiritual quest, as the energy heightens your emotional sensitivity and perception of your surroundings. Be mindful of feelings of insecurity. Should you begin to feel insecure just be patient and open to letting events unfold as they come.

SEPTEMBER 17TH: LAST QUARTER IN GEMINI

Under the Gemini moon you may find that communicating your feelings and emotions becomes easier. Your actions are motivated by the desire for variety and the urge to satisfy curiosity. Just be careful you don't become reckless and fickle – the key is harmony of the mind and heart.

SEPTEMBER 25TH: NEW MOON IN VIRGO

The Virgo moon is one of order and practicality. You feel you have to reorganize and bring order to anything you feel is in chaos. This can lead to being intolerant of others, so try focusing more on solving problems, creating order within your life, and helping others without judgement.

RITUAL PLANNER

GOAL/INTENTION:

ITEMS NEEDED:

STEPS:

SEPTEMBER HERB PLANTING GUIDE: THE COLORFUL AND CREATIVE COTTAGE GARDEN

The cottage garden design is the quintessential witch garden, in my opinion. It's creative, it's colorful, it's free and wild, and has the perfect balance of prettiness and practicality. It's the perfect design for witches because it's magical, it's useful, it's helpful, and it's beneficial to the surrounding land and local critters.

The Cottage garden originated as a means to maximize usefulness, consisting mainly of edible and medicinal plants. People without money or means to get food or medicine grew as much as they could fit within their tiny bit of land. Today, people plant cottage gardens more for pleasure and aesthetics than they do for practicality.
A cottage garden design consists of a diverse variety of plants that appeals to all senses, with pleasing aromas, bright and cheery colors, a range of textures and an assortment of shapes and sizes. The garden has an optimistic, laid back, and welcoming spirit. The plants may appear as though their seeds were mixed up and thrown into the soil at random, but placement is important. It's an organized chaos, but one that gardeners with any level of experience can achieve with a bit of consideration, contemplation, and planning.

Suggestions for Cottage Garden Creation

Based on personal experience and research, I've learned that you can create and maintain a happy and healthy cottage garden by keeping a few key suggestions in mind. First and foremost: start small! You can always add more to the garden later, but you don't want to turn half your yard into a cottage garden just to have half of it die before June. Planting in front of a picket fence or lattice slat would give the garden structure, make a picturesque backdrop, and provide the opportunity to include a climbing plant (i.e. climbing roses, wisteria, morning glories). Planting flowering shrubs, small fruit trees, or ornamental grasses would also provide structure. Adding a structural component adds a bit of order to the chaos. For enticing aromas plant a variety of herbs.

When choosing flowers, TheGardeningCook.com says that an assortment of tall flowering perennials, hardy biennials, and self-seeding annuals will "give your garden just the right look". Examples of tall flowering perennials include Bellflower, Phlox, and Delphinium; hardy biennials include Foxglove, Forget Me Nots, and Sweet William; and self-seeding annuals include Calendula, Bachelor Button, and Poppies. Repeating colors and patterns would maintain the chaotic look with

Source List/Suggested Reading:
https://www.bhg.com/gardening/yard/garden-care/cottage-garden-care/ https://www.gardendesign.com/cottage/ideas.html
https://www.thespruce.com/creating-a-cottage-garden-1402541
https://thegardeningcook.com/30-cottage-garden-plants-for-your-garden/

Record a Card Pull

DECK USED: ______________________

CARD(S) PULLED: ______________________

____

____

YOUR INTERPRETATION:

____

____

____

____

____

____

BOOK INTERPRETATION:

____

____

____

____

____

____

THE HYGGE HOMESTEAD & THE MAGIC OF COMFORT

What is Hygge?

Hygge is the practice of creating comforting and welcoming places, even in the harshest and darkest of seasons. Hygge is feeling comfortable, safe, and content in an inviting and cozy setting. Hygge, which is pronounced hoo-ga, is a practice that originated in Denmark but is honored all over Scandinavia. For people living in regions with more extended and darker winters, hygge can be a way of coping with uncomfortable weather. And this lifestyle seems to be working since Danes are commonly ranked as some of the happiest people in the world.

Bringing Hygge Into Your Heart

When trying to figure out what hygge means to you, the best first question you can ask yourself is, "what makes you feel cozy?" Coziness can be felt when we are relaxed and feeling safe when we have intimate moments with our families or friends when the troubles of the world cannot penetrate the walls of your warm and inviting home. Hygge is all about creating an atmosphere where you can quickly feel cozy. The Little Book of Hygge suggests that hygge is what we may call "hominess." I have personally found that I am experiencing hygge when I feel whole or complete, or perhaps even warm in my solar plexus and heart.

Hygge places great importance on creating this feeling for close friends and loved ones in addition to yourself. So, you may also want to ask, "what moments in my life did I feel at ease and close to others?" Hygge feels like a mindful state of authentic comfort and connection to a wholehearted present moment. Try and think about a time you felt completely at ease. Maybe you're thinking about a time you are wrapped up in a blanket enjoying a cup of tea and the company of your cat after a long day. Or perhaps you think about cooking a warm meal for your family and the feeling of eating the meal together while the snow is falling outside. These memories may be some that you hold close to your heart and, I think, show the soft power of hygge and seeking out coziness.

Bringing Hygge Into Your Home

There are many ways to make your home more hyggelig; that is, more hygge in nature. These are ways to make space feel safer, more inviting, and more comfortable. One valuable thing to keep in mind is that hygge does not need to be an expensive endeavor. If you are looking for inspiration, you will find it easily only on Pinterest boards and Tumblr.

Lighting is an essential aspect of hygge. The most revered form of this kind of lighting is the natural golden glow of candles. Luckily, most witches have a deep love for candles, so you may have plenty at home! The light and warmth of a fireplace are also rather hyggelig.

A hyggekrog is a nook in a home–this is a cozy little corner that you love to go to curl up with a book and a cup of tea. They are charming by windows, where you can look out to admire the weather and enjoy natural lighting.

Blankets, along with cushions and pillows, can make up a plush place to wrap yourself and relax.

Natural elements are celebrated in hygge and reflected through furniture and decorations. Wooden objects and plants can give off the calming feeling of being surrounded by nature.

Clean with no clutter. An area can still be complete without being cluttered. Hygge allows for meaningful and practical objects, but it is preferred to keep the space clean and organized for optimal coziness.

Hygge Activities with Others

Hygge is often linked to hospitality and creates an inviting space where you can have a close and meaningful interaction with close loved ones. One word that often comes up when considering the feeling of hygge is "togetherness." Hygge with others does not necessarily mean a massive, loud party. Instead, it is an intimate and gentle experience, creating a setting for thoughtful conversation, generosity, and the deepening of relationships. It only takes a few close friends or family members, and the magic number for shared hygge seems to be three or four people. One easy hygge activity is eating together. There are plenty of foods associated with hygge, some of them being cake, cinnamon rolls, soups, and hot drinks. Other activities for hygge include playing board games or telling stories around a fire.

For witches, I suggest some of the following activities that may conjure hygge:
Reading divination together around a candlelit table.
Writing in a book of shadows together.
Creating a magical dish of food to share.
Another fun activity could be a magical gift swap. For this, each guest is asked to bring a magical item they can use in the craft that can be shared and exchanged with someone else.

Solo Hygge Activities

Hygge is something that can be felt privately in solitary moments as well. If you are an introvert like me, there is comfort and recovery in alone time. There are plenty of hyggelig activities that you can enjoy alone: reading, writing, drawing, knitting, building a scrapbook, enjoying a hot bath, and observing the weather are a few to consider. You may discover that hygge activities center around savoring the present moment as an opportunity to honor peace and mindfulness. For witches, I suggest reading Norse mythology or Danish folklore, reading magical books, meditating, reading divination for yourself, enjoying a comforting meal while watching a movie or show on witchcraft, or trying some cozy magic.

Cozy Magic

Here are some magical ideas to bring coziness and hygge into your life this winter season.

Warming Visualization: Close your eyes and take long, slow, deep breaths. Try and focus on your breath, and when your mind drifts, just gently return to the rhythm of your breathing. When you breathe in, imagine with your mind's eye that your heart is giving off a warm, comforting golden light. As you feel your breath fill your lungs, imagine the light getting brighter. When you breathe out, imagine this golden light moving through your body, warming up and comforting your body. If you have specific areas that are tense or sore, send the warmth to those places. This simple practice can be done for a couple of minutes or for as long as you please. You can also use this visualization for peace, healing, and comfort magic.

Blanket or Sweater Spell: Enchant your favorite blanket or sweater with healing energies, peace, safety, and security. You may want to hold the blanket or sweater and envision that once you are wrapped in it or wearing it, you are safe from the troubles of the outside world and at ease to feel wellness and contentment.

Hearth Altar: If you are fortunate to have a fireplace in your home, use the hearth as a place to stage a Hygge altar. Objects you may want to include are candles, an oil diffuser, ceramic containers, or vintage trinkets.

Candle Spells: Since candles are a centerpiece for hygge, a candle spell may be an excellent activity to conjure comfort. A simple comfort candle spell calls for a white candle. Dress the candle in cardamom and vanilla essential oils. Light the candle and take a moment to observe the flame, contemplating the sensation of hygge. Repeat the following chant, or use one of your own:
My home is a place of comfort and ease.
It is safe and conjures peace.
All who come here feel relief in this place.
May this candle conjure relaxing energy in this space.

Bibliography

Altman, Anna. "The Year of Hygge, The Danish Obsession with Getting Cozy." The New Yorker. Newyorker.com. Published 18 DEC 16. Accessed 15 JAN 20.
Edberg, Pia. The Cozy Life: Rediscover the Joy of the Simple Things Through the Danish Concept of Hygge. Self-Published, 2016.
James, Ryan and Amy White. Hygge: An Introduction to the Danish Art of Cozy Living. Self Published, 2017.
Soderberg, Marie Tourell. Hygge: The Danish Art of Happiness. Penguin Books:
Wiking, Meik. The Little Book of Hygge: Danish Secrets to Happy Living. Harper Collins, NY, 2017.

PAUSE & REFLECT

Do you currently have a talisman or good luck charm? If so, what is it and why? If not, what would you look for in one?

SEPTEMBER FESTIVALS

The 15th day of the 8th month of the Chinese lunisolar calendar, (which falls in either September or November of the Gregorian calendar), the Moon festival is celebrated by people of East and Southeast Asia. The Moon festival, or the Mid-Autumn Festival, originated 3000 years ago when the Chinese worshipped the moon, revering it as a symbol of peace and prosperity, and held the festival to gain the moons' blessing for a bountiful harvest. Today, the Moon Festival is celebrated by carrying or displaying lanterns of all shapes and sizes as symbolic beacons, guiding people towards prosperity and good fortune. The traditional food of the Moon festival is the moon cake, which is a pastry filled with either sweet-bean or lotus-seed paste.
The Moon festival is known as Chuseok, "Autumn Eve", in Korea (both North and South), Tsukimi, "Moon Viewing", in Japan, and Tét Trung Thu, "Mid-Autumn Festival", in Vietnam.
[Source: https://en.wikipedia.org/wiki/Mid-Autumn_Festival]

USE THE SPACE BELOW TO RECORD YOUR SEPTEMBER CELEBRATIONS

5 SEPTEMBER
MONDAY

6 SEPTEMBER
TUESDAY

9 SEPTEMBER
FRIDAY

10 SEPTEMBER
SATURDAY

7 SEPTEMBER
WEDNESDAY

8 SEPTEMBER
THURSDAY

11 SEPTEMBER
SUNDAY

SEPTEMBER - 2022

	M	T	W	T	F	S	S
35	29	30	31	1	2	3	4
36	5	6	7	8	9	10	11
37	12	13	14	15	16	17	18
38	19	20	21	22	23	24	25
39	26	27	28	29	30	1	2

12 SEPTEMBER
MONDAY

13 SEPTEMBER
TUESDAY

16 SEPTEMBER
FRIDAY

17 SEPTEMBER
SATURDAY

14 SEPTEMBER
WEDNESDAY

15 SEPTEMBER
THURSDAY

18 SEPTEMBER
SUNDAY

SEPTEMBER - 2022

	M	T	W	T	F	S	S
35	29	30	31	1	2	3	4
36	5	6	7	8	9	10	11
37	12	13	14	15	16	17	18
38	19	20	21	22	23	24	25
39	26	27	28	29	30	1	2

19 SEPTEMBER
MONDAY

20 SEPTEMBER
TUESDAY

23 SEPTEMBER
FRIDAY

24 SEPTEMBER
SATURDAY

21 SEPTEMBER
WEDNESDAY

22 SEPTEMBER
THURSDAY

25 SEPTEMBER
SUNDAY

SEPTEMBER - 2022

	M	T	W	T	F	S	S
35	29	30	31	1	2	3	4
36	5	6	7	8	9	10	11
37	12	13	14	15	16	17	18
38	19	20	21	22	23	24	25
39	26	27	28	29	30	1	2

26 SEPTEMBER
MONDAY

27 SEPTEMBER
TUESDAY

30 SEPTEMBER
FRIDAY

1 OCTOBER
SATURDAY

28 SEPTEMBER
WEDNESDAY

29 SEPTEMBER
THURSDAY

2 OCTOBER
SUNDAY

SEPTEMBER - 2022

	M	T	W	T	F	S	S
35	29	30	31	1	2	3	4
36	5	6	7	8	9	10	11
37	12	13	14	15	16	17	18
38	19	20	21	22	23	24	25
39	26	27	28	29	30	1	2

GRATITUDE LIST

MONTHLY TO-DO'S

TRY SOMETHING NEW

CRYSTALS

Carnelian is known as the stone of motivation and endurance, leadership and courage. It's fiery energies of the rising sun embolden us, emblazing our passions. Said to attract prosperity and good luck, this is an excellent stone to carry with you to work, job interview, even a big date.

Source: https://www.crystalvaults.com/crystal-encyclopedia/carnelian

CARD SPREAD

Card 1: What you are ignoring - Card 2: What you are obsessing over - Card 3: What you need to focus on

SPELL: Aries Motivation Spell

When the moon moves into Aries, take a red candle to the windowsill and set it in the moonlight – or lack thereof if it's a new moon. When you feel it's charged fully with that fiery Aries energy, take a pin or something sharp and carve your name in the side of the candle. Think about what your goal, and when you have one in your mind carve a symbol or sigil into the other side of the candle that represents your goal. Even if you don't have a goal in mind, you will still bring Aries' motivational energy to you.

Light the candle and let the energy release, knowing you'll be motivated to do what you need to in short time. You can snuff the candle and relight it as often as you need to – just don't leave it burning unattended!

ENTITY

Clean the frames of your loved one's photos.

SELF-CARE

Delete those 10,000 emails, if you haven't read them now, you never will.

TEA

Rooibos Tea - Also known as Red Tea, this is an herbal plant that grows in South Africa. Perfect for tea lovers looking to reduce caffeine intake.

HERBS

Before we had antibiotic ointment and healing balms, we had poultices. Herbs for healing, especially those with anti-inflammatory and antiseptic properties, are crushed, smeared onto a warm, wet cloth, and applied to the afflicted area (i.e. burns, cuts, bruises, aches and pains).

Record a Card Pull

DECK USED:

CARD(S) PULLED:

YOUR INTERPRETATION:

BOOK INTERPRETATION:

"Witchcraft is never cookie-cutter. Like recipes from a book, the recipes are often tailored to individual tastes as long as the general formula and steps are understood."

-Mat Auryn, Psychic Witch: A Metaphysical Guide to Meditation, Magick & Manifestation

MONDAY	TUESDAY	WEDNESDAY	THURSDAY
3	4	5	6
10	11	12	13
17	18	19	20
24 / Samhain 31	25	26	27

Calendar Key

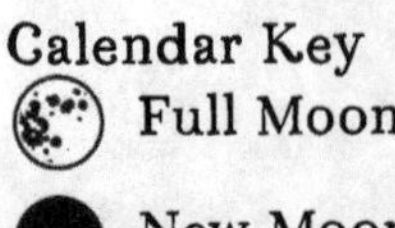
Full Moon
New Moon

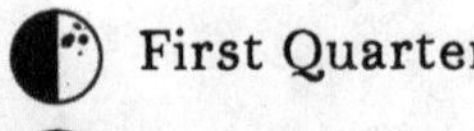
First Quarter
Last Quarter

Eclipse
Sun

FRIDAY	SATURDAY	SUNDAY
	1	♑ 2
7	8	♈ 9
14	15	16
21	22	♏ 23
28	29	30

OCT

goals

OCTOBER

M	T	W	T	F	S	S
26	27	28	29	30	1	2
3	4	5	6	7	8	9
10	11	12	13	14	15	16
17	18	19	20	21	22	23
24	25	26	27	28	29	30
31	1	2	3	4	5	6

LUNAR PHASES

OCTOBER 2ND: FIRST QUARTER IN CAPRICORN

The moon in Capricorn has an emotional seriousness, a sober orientation, and a practical awareness that brings with it a need to feel useful. Using the energies of the new moon and amplified ambitions of Capricorn, this is an ideal time to start new projects.

OCTOBER 9TH: FULL MOON IN ARIES

The moon in Aries is emotionally direct and impulsive, with strong, influential feelings. Time for a fresh start, learning new behaviors, establishing new habits. Just don't rush to make decisions, as Aries is apt to do, feeling as though quicker is better. It's not. Take your time to consider what you need, what you want, and choose carefully. The choices made in Aries set the tone for the extended future.

OCTOBER 17TH: LAST QUARTER IN CANCER

The Moon in Cancer instills in you emotional security and a sense of belonging, a sense of nurturing you feel instinctively. You find that you're longing for an intimate connection that's meaningful and long-lasting, enough so you can establish a sense of belonging-put down roots, a place to bunker down as the Universe throws its' trials and tribulations at you. Using the Full Moon energies to work a self-love spell may help to satisfy this desire.

OCTOBER 25TH: NEW MOON IN SCORPIO (PARTIAL SOLAR ECLIPSE)

Scorpio energy encourages us to explore our feelings more deeply, and we find we're drawn to sex, power and money. Learning what gets other people going is arousing. Instinctive orientation

RITUAL PLANNER

GOAL/INTENTION:

ITEMS NEEDED:

STEPS:

THE SILENT SUPPER: A FEAST FOR ANCESTORS

Suppose you are looking for a profound way to honor your ancestors while dining. In that case, the Silent Supper may be a supernatural and magical activity to try out. The Silent Supper, sometimes known as the Silent Supper, is a special meal that is prepared, arranged, and served with an extra special guest: the spirit of someone close to you who has passed over. The premise of the Silent Supper is simple:
-Create a delectable feast.
-Set an extra place for the spirit you are commemorating.
-Have the meal in silence.

The word "Silent" is used to refer to the fact that the meal takes place in complete silence. While a Silent Supper can technically be hosted at any time, it is commonly associated with the season of Samhain, when we honor ancestors and the world of the dead. Here are a few additional ideas that can help you plan for hosting a Silent Supper.

The History of the Silent Supper

While modern Pagans and witches have revered the Silent Supper as a tradition to feast with the dearly departed, the Silent Supper has folkloric roots in love divination. There is little evidence to even indicate that the Silent Supper had ancient origins, deeply seeded in a distant Pagan World. That being said, what we do see historically is still fascinating and worth considering.

The accounts of the divinatory Silent Supper have appeared in the British Isles and America. However, many Silent Supper games have been connected to Appalachian and Ozark regions, especially in rural locations during Victorian times. Two unmarried young ladies would sweep, clean, cook, sit at the table and wait in silence. At the end of the meal, it was believed that the vision of a person would clearly appear – this person would be one of the ladies' future mates. Other accounts say that the future husband would walk through the door at midnight. This Silent Supper has come with a range of strange procedures for participants to see results, including doing activities backward (such as serving dessert first), preparing food behind your back, and even throwing freshly clipped nails into a fire. Some even warned that seeing a coffin at the end of the Silent Supper was an unfortunate omen of death. While modern Pagans have created the Silent Supper into a more reverent ritual than a divination game, both versions still possess a supernatural energy. However, the contemporary rendition focuses on honoring the Dead, celebrating their memories, and possibly having a spiritual encounter with them.

Honoring the Dead

Before you begin to prepare for your Silent Supper, consider someone who has passed away that you would like to honor. Know that they are coming to have dinner with you in spirit, so consider what you would like to do in their presence and why you wish to have them present. And, a special note: you are certainly welcome to invite dearly departed pets. Anyone who has lost a loved pet knows that they are also special and vital family members.

Preparing Your Space and Table Settings

Have a tidy and clean space to host the meal – if you chose to, consider purifying the space with incense or wiping the table with rose water. Use this special feast as an opportunity to express your decorative spirit. If you are hosting this during the Samhain season, incorporate symbols that you associate with your Samhain practices, for example, pumpkins and black or orange candles. This is also your opportunity to include decorations you associate with the person you honor for the feast. This could mean decorating with photos of the person or even featuring personal effects, like jewelry or their heirloom dining ware. Assign seating ahead of time, ensuring that one seat is left for the spirit you honor at the meal.

The Food and Offerings

It has always been said that you should prepare the favorite foods of the person you are honoring at the Silent Supper. Think about what you would cook for them if they were alive. If you are honoring someone who was a cook while alive, consider using his/her/their personal recipes. You may also want to consider including additional offerings to welcome the people you are honoring. This may include a favorite beverage prepared to their liking, cigarettes or tobacco, flowers, or special personal items that you've crafted. If you are preparing a space for dear pets who have passed over, consider where they feel most welcome. You may have an old feeding dish or favorite blanket that you can set up in a cozy spot for your pet to also feel welcome to visit. Consider welcoming them with a favorite toy or treat or a particular food item they enjoyed on special occasions while alive.

The Silent Supper

The Silent Supper should be a calmer event. Not one could be interrupted with high energy, distractions, or loud noises. The Silent Supper itself has been described in a variety of ways - perhaps you can determine which method feels suitable for your celebration. The traditional method used for a Silent Supper is to have the meal in complete silence. This is said to be a way to show reverence for those who have passed away. This serves as a time to quietly reflect on the person who passed and as an opportunity to listen for any sounds that would indicate the spirit being present.
In contrast, some believe that the Silent Supper has moments of conversation and sound. There may be times where favorite music is played, or favorite memories and funny stories are shared. Perhaps these conversations can be had as a way to open the meal or to close the feast. While there are silent moments, see if you experience anything that would indicate that a spirit is present. Perhaps there is a temperature change, or you smell their favorite perfume. Maybe you hear knocks, distant laughter, or a comforting word to ease your heart in

knowing they are with you.

Closing the Feast

You may find it appropriate to have a special closing ritual after the dinner is done. You may wish to ask everyone around the table to say thank you and a personal message to the spirits in attendance. You may want to ring a bell or share in a song, incantation, or prayer together. Some believe the best way to close the Silent Supper is with a delightful dessert or comforting dinner rolls. However you plan your Silent Supper, know that it is a beautiful ritual to show your appreciation for those you love, miss, and respect.

Record a Card Pull

DECK USED:

CARD(S) PULLED:

YOUR INTERPRETATION:

BOOK INTERPRETATION:

OCTOBER HERB GUIDE

Herbs for Psychic Ability and Divination

Psychic work and divination are a major aspect of witchcraft, and it's helpful to know which herbs will aid you in your psychic endeavors. The herbs listed above all classify as psychic herbs, each having properties that allow for a range of magical workings. Burn dried yarrow to cleanse your divination tools or create a sacred space.

Create a sachet of amethyst and borage to instill courage when trying a new form of divination, while pennyroyal can be used to prepare yourself for divination or spirit work. Blue vervain added to a bath or made into a tea (use food grade only) will help open your Third Eye and amplify your psychic abilities.

ERB	SIZE/ SPREAD	START SEEDS INSIDE/OUTSIDE	HARDINESS ZONE	NATIVE REGION	GROWTH TYPE**	SUN/- SOIL**
lue rvain	1-2'/1-2'	2-3 mos. (Stratified*) 70° soil/NR	3-10	Wet regions of Missouri	A, P	FS/WD
rrow	6"-3'/2-3'	6-8/After Last Frost	3-9	North America, Europe, Asia	P	FS/LS
rage	1-3'/6-18"	3-4/3-4 After	2-11	Mediterranean	A	PS/R
nyroyal	12-18"/18"	8-10/3-4	5-9	Europe, Middle East, North Africa	P	FS,PS/ ML
eeks before or afer last spring frost						
=Annual P=Perennial						
S= full sun, PS= partial sun; WD= well-drained, M= moist, RM, rich moint, L= loamy, LS=loamy/sandy						

Blue Vervain: Known as a psychic herb, associated with the moon. Enhance divination and psychic dreaming
Yarrow: Enhance divination and psychic work, protection against negative energies, prophetic magic, clear blockages, enhance creativity
Borrage: Courage, psychic powers, protection, Air magic
Pennyroyal: Protection of psychic energy against negative influences, strengthen and heal Aura, clear chakra blockages

PAUSE & REFLECT

Do you currently feel blessed or cursed?

OCTOBER FESTIVALS

Dziady is a Slavic holiday concerning the spirits of ancestors that dates back to pre-Christian times. Dziady translates to "Forefathers Eve", the intention of the holiday being communion of the living with the dead or establishing of relationships with the spirits of your ancestors. The holiday of Dziady occurred twice a year: Spring Dziady, from the last day of April to the first day of May, and Autumn Dziady, from the last day of October to the first day of November. It was believed that these were the two days the spirits of the dead were able to return to earth. By establishing yourself as a host, you would secure the favor of the spirit as well as help them find peace once their assistance was no longer required. The ritual of Dziady consisted of eating a feast specially prepared either in your home or at the cemetery on the grave of the spirit you wish to host. While eating, people would drop bits of food and pour some of their drink onto the table or the grave, as offerings for the spirits which you could not clear or remove until the holiday had passed. In some areas the ritual included preparing a bath for the spirit, which was achieved by warming up the sauna or lighting a fire, which provided light to guide them towards you. In modern day practices, this aspect of the ritual is satisfied by lighting candles on the grave.
[Source: https://en.wikipedia.org/wiki/Dziady]

USE THE SPACE BELOW TO RECORD YOUR OCTOBER CELEBRATIONS

3 OCTOBER
MONDAY

4 OCTOBER
TUESDAY

7 OCTOBER
FRIDAY

8 OCTOBER
SATURDAY

5 OCTOBER
WEDNESDAY

6 OCTOBER
THURSDAY

9 OCTOBER
SUNDAY

OCTOBER - 2022

	M	T	W	T	F	S	S
39	26	27	28	29	30	1	2
40	3	4	5	6	7	8	9
41	10	11	12	13	14	15	16
42	17	18	19	20	21	22	23
43	24	25	26	27	28	29	30
44	31	1	2	3	4	5	6

10 OCTOBER
MONDAY

11 OCTOBER
TUESDAY

14 OCTOBER
FRIDAY

15 OCTOBER
SATURDAY

12 OCTOBER
WEDNESDAY

13 OCTOBER
THURSDAY

16 OCTOBER
SUNDAY

OCTOBER - 2022

	M	T	W	T	F	S	S
39	26	27	28	29	30	1	2
40	3	4	5	6	7	8	9
41	10	11	12	13	14	15	16
42	17	18	19	20	21	22	23
43	24	25	26	27	28	29	30
44	31	1	2	3	4	5	6

17 OCTOBER
MONDAY

18 OCTOBER
TUESDAY

21 OCTOBER
FRIDAY

22 OCTOBER
SATURDAY

19 OCTOBER
WEDNESDAY

20 OCTOBER
THURSDAY

23 OCTOBER
SUNDAY

OCTOBER - 2022

	M	T	W	T	F	S	S
39	26	27	28	29	30	1	2
40	3	4	5	6	7	8	9
41	10	11	12	13	14	15	16
42	17	18	19	20	21	22	23
43	24	25	26	27	28	29	30
44	31	1	2	3	4	5	6

24 OCTOBER
MONDAY

25 OCTOBER
TUESDAY

28 OCTOBER
FRIDAY

29 OCTOBER
SATURDAY

26 OCTOBER
WEDNESDAY

27 OCTOBER
THURSDAY

30 OCTOBER
SUNDAY

OCTOBER - 2022

	M	T	W	T	F	S	S
39	26	27	28	29	30	1	2
40	3	4	5	6	7	8	9
41	10	11	12	13	14	15	16
42	17	18	19	20	21	22	23
43	24	25	26	27	28	29	30
44	31	1	2	3	4	5	6

GRATITUDE LIST

MONTHLY TO-DO'S

TRY SOMETHING NEW

CRYSTALS

Crystal Infused water, or gem water, is a must-have for any witch's magical tool cabinet. To make gem water, you simply add cleansed and charged crystals to water, then set the bowl or jar under a luminary source to charge. If you set in the sun, leave it for about three hours, and leave overnight if you use the new or full moon. If the crystal you wish to use cannot be put into water, you may still use the gem to make the water. Just put the crystals in a smaller bowl and float the bowl in the water, or put the crystals in a water tight bag and lower the bag into the water, just remove it before storing the water. Keep gem water in a cool, dark cabinet in a spray bottle or jar. Uses: anoint candles, anoint yourself, spritz around the room, your car, use for cleaning or cleansing. Add to potions or bath. (check to make sure the crystal is safe for use on or in the body).

Source: https://wiccanow.com/how-to-make-crystal-infused-water/

CARD SPREAD

Card 1: Message from an Ancestor - Card 2: Message from a Spirit - Card 3: Message from a Guide

SPELL: Travel Protection Sachet

Draw Down the Sun for Seasonal Depression: The winters in the north of the US can be brutal and often people are afflicted with depression. To melt those cold, blue feelings away, step outside and find a nice sunny spot to stand in. Just as you draw down the moon, you will draw down the energy of the sun into your body. You will feel rejuvenated, energetic, creative -just all around happy for the day. I bring out a necklace or ring with me when I do this, to charge them with the suns' energy so I have a sun energy amulet on hand. You can say an incantation, but it's not necessary. Just close your eyes, tilt your head back and stretch your arms open and out. Feel a beam of energy reach out from the sun and down until it reaches you. The beam will enter your body through your core, where your solar plexus is. Stand there until you feel filled head to toe with warm, golden energy.

ENTITY

Host a silent supper: create a nice meal and set your table leaving a chair and plate available for the dead.

SELF-CARE

Get a frappuccino today- no one will judge you.

TEA

PSL Tea - Black tea blended with clove, cinnamon, cardamom, and nutmeg with a splash of steam milk with remind you for your favorite coffee shop latte.

HERBS

The clove, or the Syzgium aromaticum, should be a staple in any witches apothecary. This aromatic herb is great for magic involving luck, money/ prosperity, keeping good friends close and enemies at bay, stops gossip, and in sex magic, as they are an aphrodisiac.

Record a Card Pull

DECK USED:

CARD(S) PULLED:

YOUR INTERPRETATION:

BOOK INTERPRETATION:

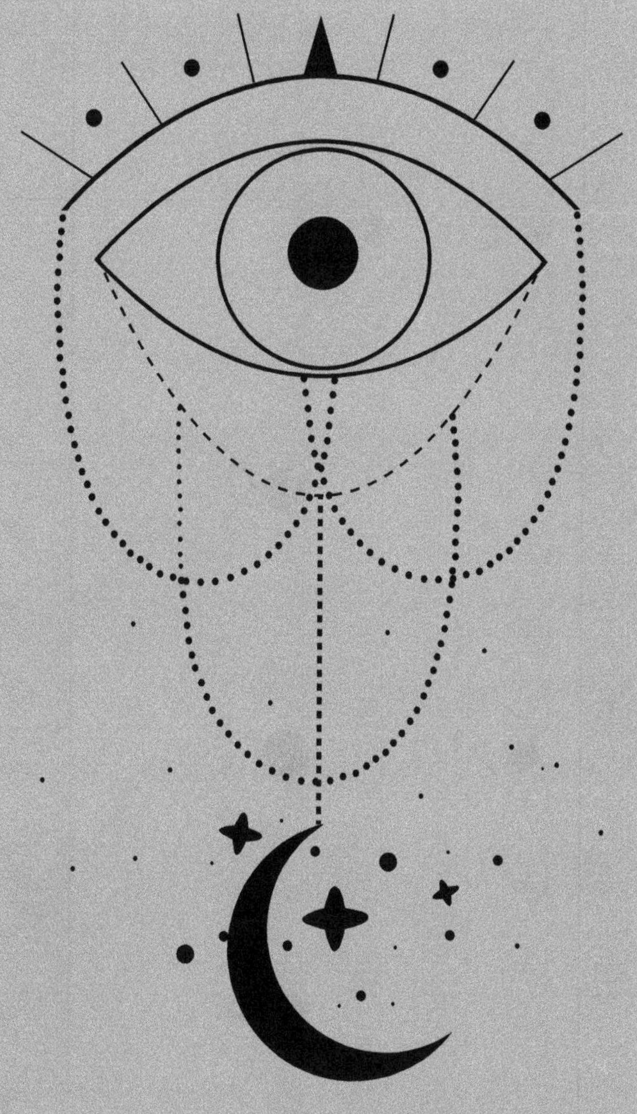

"Visualization is the main ingredient of magic, inner peace: power."

- Jessica Marie Baumgartner,

MONDAY	TUESDAY	WEDNESDAY	THURSDAY
31	1	2	3
7	8	9	10
14	15	16	17
21	22	23	24
28	29	30	

Calendar Key

Full Moon

First Quarter

Eclipse

New Moon

Last Quarter

Sun

FRIDAY	SATURDAY	SUNDAY
4	5	6
11	12	13
18	19	20
25	26	27

NOV

goals

NOVEMBER

	M	T	W	T	F	S	S
44	31	1	2	3	4	5	6
45	7	8	9	10	11	12	13
46	14	15	16	17	18	19	20
47	21	22	23	24	25	26	27
48	28	29	30	1	2	3	4

LUNAR PHASES

NOVEMBER 1ST: FIRST QUARTER IN AQUARIUS

The moon in Aquarius gives us the need for emotional freedoms which can cause complications in our relationships. Can also be a time when you are able to better understand your emotions, freeing you from negative feelings such as jealousy, fear, and anger.

NOVEMBER 8TH: FULL MOON IN TAURUS (LUNAR ECLIPSE)

Your sense of safety arises from the need for stability which is difficult to find at the moment. The key to stability is acceptance - accepting that change is a part of life, and acceptance of who you are as a person. When you accept yourself you will find that peace and tranquility are much easier to come by in your daily life.

NOVEMBER 16TH: LAST QUARTER IN LEO

Impressing others and receiving praise will give you a sense of safety and sevurity while the moon is in Leo. This only sets you up for failure, as you'll find yourself at a loss as soon as you're put in the spotlight. The key to navigating through Leo is accepting that feedback and criticism are useful, they help you improve. The first step to accepting these facts is to admit you are afraid of criticism, and to admit that you can't accept criticism. Only once you admit the truth of the problem can you work through it.

NOVEMBER 23RD: NEW MOON IN SCORPIO

Scorpio energy encourages us to explore our feelings more deeply, and we find we're drawn to sex, power and money. Learning what gets other people going is arousing. Instinctive orientation is to start over from scratch. Only by destroying the roots of disturbances can you begin healing.

NOVEMBER 30TH: FIRST QUARTER IN PISCES

The moon in Pisces is a great time for a creative or spiritual quest, as the energy heightens your emotional sensitivity and perception of your surroundings. Be mindful of feelings of insecurity. Should you begin to feel insecure just be patient and open to letting events unfold as they come.

RITUAL PLANNER

GOAL/INTENTION:

ITEMS NEEDED:

STEPS:

PROPELLED BY PASSION: CALLING ON CERRIDWEN TO ACHIEVE YOUR GOALS

The Tale of Gwion Bach[1]

The goddess Cerridwen gave birth to a son, Morfran, but to her dismay, he was terrifyingly ugly. When people started calling him Afagddu, meaning utter darkness, Cerridwen turned to divination to find a way to get her son accepted and respected in society. She learned of a potion that had to be boiled for a year and a day that required the magic of the herbs of the earth and human effort. Cerridwen enlisted a blind old man to stir the brew, and a young boy, Gwion Bach, to stoke the fire, while she traveled far and wide collecting the herbs. When the potion was complete, three drops would jump out, bestowing the gifts of wisdom, prophecy and storytelling upon whomever they landed.

When the year and day had passed, Cerridwen brought her son over to the cauldron and laid down to sleep. However, just as the three drops jumped from the cauldron, Gwion pushed Morfran out of the way and they landed on Gwion Bach. An instant later the remaining brew turned into a noxious poison so potent the cauldron shattered and woke Cerridwen. When she saw what had happened, she was furious. Gwion, knowing her venomous fury, turned himself into a hare and darted away. Cerridwen turned into a greyhound and pursued Gwion.

Gwion turned into a salmon, so Cerridwen turned into an otter. Gwion then turned into a bird to fly away, so Cerridwen shifted into a hawk. Gwion decided to try hiding so he turned into a grain of wheat. Cerridwen shifted into a hen and ate him, and a moment later became pregnant with him. Cerridwen resolved to kill him once he was born, but when the time came, she didn't have the heart to hurt him and sent him floating down a river. That baby grew up to be the bard Taliesin- "he with the radiant brow".

[1]Retelling of the myth as described in From the Cauldron Born: Exploring the Magic of Welsh Legend & Lore by Kristoffer Hughes (2012, Llewellyn Publications)

Magic, Transformation, and Strong-willed Determination

While this tale tells of magic and transformation, there is an underlying lesson of passion, endurance, and strong-willed determination. Cerridwen went to the ends of the earth to help her son and did so again to serve what she believed to be justice. Meditate upon the Tale of Gwion Bach and consider what you would have done in her place.

If, as the autumn season wanes, you find your pace slowing, your determination to achieve your goals draining, call upon Cerridwen to help you divine your path, as well as teach you how to build up your endurance and strengthen your determination. Build an altar for her, following your instincts when choosing decorations and tools. My only suggestions would be to include the symbol of Awen and to use a cauldron, dedicated to Cerridwen, to hold your offerings to her.

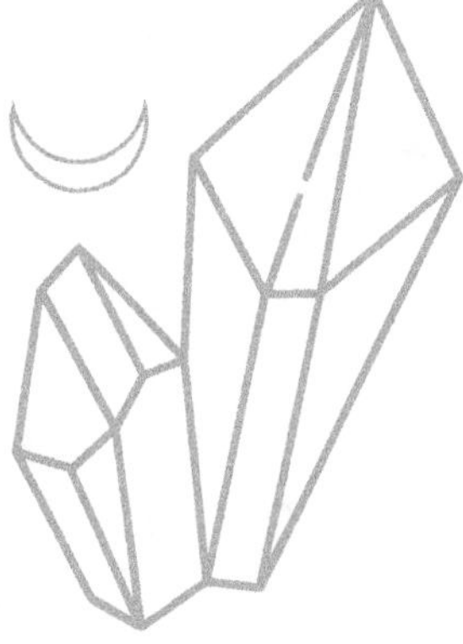

PAUSE & REFLECT

What is the biggest lesson you've learned so far in life?

NOVEMBER FESTIVALS

The northern region of the town Man, located on the Ivory Coast of Africa, plays host to the Festival of Masks. Every November, people from neighboring villages gather together in celebration, dancing and dressed in elaborate masks and colorful costumes. The masks are custom made to embody forest spirits, which are then honored by the dancing and festivities. The neighboring villages hold contests, naming the best dancers. This Festival of Masks is important to the Ivory Coast because it helps unify the region, which has been rife with violence and divided by civil war that has been on-going since 2002. Organizers of the Festival of Masks aim to preserve the culture shared by the diverse population by encouraging unity through the revival of the mask tradition.
[Source: https://www.iexplore.com/articles/travel-guides/africa/cote-divoire/festivals-and-events, https://www.voanews.com/archive/mask-festival-helps-unify-ivory-coast]

USE THE SPACE BELOW TO RECORD YOUR NOVEMBER CELEBRATIONS

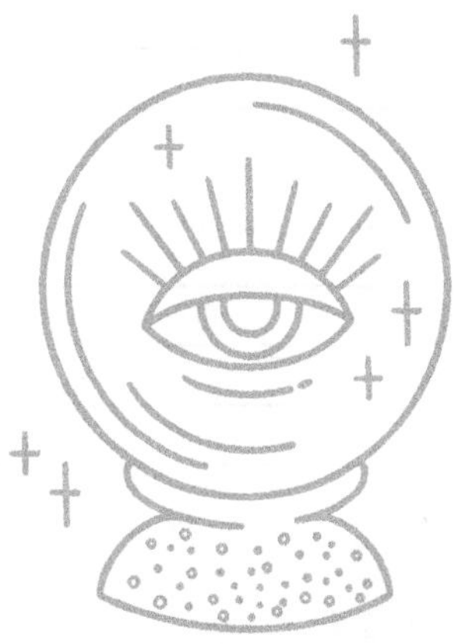

31 OCTOBER
MONDAY

1 NOVEMBER
TUESDAY

4 NOVEMBER
FRIDAY

5 NOVEMBER
SATURDAY

2 NOVEMBER
WEDNESDAY

3 NOVEMBER
THURSDAY

6 NOVEMBER
SUNDAY

NOVEMBER - 2022

	M	T	W	T	F	S	S
44	31	1	2	3	4	5	6
45	7	8	9	10	11	12	13
46	14	15	16	17	18	19	20
47	21	22	23	24	25	26	27
48	28	29	30	1	2	3	4

7 NOVEMBER
MONDAY

8 NOVEMBER
TUESDAY

11 NOVEMBER
FRIDAY

12 NOVEMBER
SATURDAY

9 NOVEMBER
WEDNESDAY

10 NOVEMBER
THURSDAY

13 NOVEMBER
SUNDAY

NOVEMBER - 2022

	M	T	W	T	F	S	S
44	31	1	2	3	4	5	6
45	7	8	9	10	11	12	13
46	14	15	16	17	18	19	20
47	21	22	23	24	25	26	27
48	28	29	30	1	2	3	4

14 NOVEMBER
MONDAY

15 NOVEMBER
TUESDAY

18 NOVEMBER
FRIDAY

19 NOVEMBER
SATURDAY

16 NOVEMBER
WEDNESDAY

17 NOVEMBER
THURSDAY

20 NOVEMBER
SUNDAY

NOVEMBER - 2022

	M	T	W	T	F	S	S
44	31	1	2	3	4	5	6
45	7	8	9	10	11	12	13
46	14	15	16	17	18	19	20
47	21	22	23	24	25	26	27
48	28	29	30	1	2	3	4

21 NOVEMBER
MONDAY

22 NOVEMBER
TUESDAY

25 NOVEMBER
FRIDAY

26 NOVEMBER
SATURDAY

23 NOVEMBER
WEDNESDAY

24 NOVEMBER
THURSDAY

27 NOVEMBER
SUNDAY

NOVEMBER - 2022

	M	T	W	T	F	S	S
44	31	1	2	3	4	5	6
45	7	8	9	10	11	12	13
46	14	15	16	17	18	19	20
47	21	22	23	24	25	26	27
48	28	29	30	1	2	3	4

28 NOVEMBER
MONDAY

29 NOVEMBER
TUESDAY

2 DECEMBER
FRIDAY

3 DECEMBER
SATURDAY

30 NOVEMBER
WEDNESDAY

1 DECEMBER
THURSDAY

4 DECEMBER
SUNDAY

DECEMBER - 2022

	M	T	W	T	F	S	S
48	28	29	30	1	2	3	4
49	5	6	7	8	9	10	11
50	12	13	14	15	16	17	18
51	19	20	21	22	23	24	25
52	26	27	28	29	30	31	1

GRATITUDE LIST

MONTHLY TO-DO'S

TRY SOMETHING NEW

CRYSTALS:
Blue Chalcedony is a member of the quartz family is known as the “speakers’ stone”, for its’ ability to ease fears of public speaking, instilling courage to release words that normally get stuck in your throat, and can aid in pathworking, allowing for clear communication with Spirit. It’s said that the great Roman orator, Cicero, wore a Blue Chalcedony stone on a necklace.

CARD SPREAD
Card 1: What to meditate on - Card 2: What to bring into the home - Card 3: What to take a break from

SPELL
Predicting Babies: This bit of magic has been done by all the women in my family (on my mother’s side) – it’s another Acadian tradition passed down from my great-grandmother who left French Canada in the 1800’s. There are two ways to do this – the first is to find out how many kids you’ll have and what the sex will be, the second is to do when you’re pregnant to find out the sex of the baby. As far as I know it has always been right. Thread a needle, pulling the needle to the mid-point of the thread, bring the ends together and tie them off. Hold out your dominant hand palm up, and with the other hand hold the thread, being as still as possible. It’s said that if the needle moves in a circle you’ll have a female, and side to side is a male. When my mother did this, the needle moved in a circle, then side to side, then in a circle again before coming to a stop. I’m the eldest, then I have a brother, and we have a baby sister. If it doesn’t move, don’t worry though, it just means you haven’t made the choices you’ll need to to take you down a path that leads to kids, but it doesn’t mean you won’t have kids if you want them. I know that because it happened to me, but I’m now a mother of a very energetic, social, intelligent 5 year-old-boy. When you become pregnant, lay down and have someone hold the thread above your belly. The needle will start moving and, as before, if it moves in a circle it predicts a female, and side to side it’s a male.

ENTITY
Fill your space this month with photos of friends that has passed to honor their memory.

SELF-CARE
Clean out your cabinets - I know, you hate it. Trust me, you’ll be happy you did.

TEA: Warming Tonic Tea - When the winter cold hits a tea blended with hibiscus, elderberry, and rose hips will fill you with warm antioxidants.

HERBS
Lemongrass has the subtle scent of lemons, and a decoction of lemongrass is a wonderful ingredient for cleaning potions. Lemongrass possesses several magical properties: communication, protection, love, purification, expelling negative energy, achieving, and maintaining balance, enhancing psychic power, aids with divination and brings clarity.

Record a Card Pull

DECK USED:

CARD(S) PULLED:

YOUR INTERPRETATION:

BOOK INTERPRETATION:

"The witch is notorious shape-shifter and comes in many guises. More than anything, though, the witch is a shifting and shadowy symbol of female power and a force for subverting the status quo. She is also a vessel that contains our conflicting feelings about female power: our fear of it, our desire for it, our hope that it can and will grow stronger despite the flames that are thrown at it."

- Pam Grossman, Waking the Witch: Reflections on Women, Magic, and Power

MONDAY	TUESDAY	WEDNESDAY	THURSDAY
			1
5	6	7	♊ 8
12	13	14	15
19	20	Winter Solstice/Yule 21	♑ 22
26	27	28	29

Calendar Key

Full Moon

New Moon

 First Quarter

 Last Quarter

 Eclipse

 Sun

DEC

FRIDAY	SATURDAY	SUNDAY
2	3	4
9	10	11
♍ 16	17	18
♑ 23	24	25
♈ 30	31	

goals

DECEMBER

M	T	W	T	F	S	S
28	29	30	1	2	3	4
5	6	7	8	9	10	11
12	13	14	15	16	17	18
19	20	21	22	23	24	25
26	27	28	29	30	31	1

LUNAR PHASES

DECEMBER 8TH: FULL MOON IN GEMINI

Under the Gemini moon you may find that communicating your feelings and emotions becomes easier. Your actions are motivated by the desire for variety and the urge to satisfy curiosity. Just be careful you don't become reckless and fickle – the key is harmony of the mind and heart.

DECEMBER 16TH: LAST QUARTER IN VIRGO

The Virgo moon is one of order and practicality. You feel you have to reorganize and bring order to anything you feel is in chaos. This can lead to being intolerant of others, so try focusing more on solving problems, creating order within your life, and helping others without judgement.

DECEMBER 23RD: NEW MOON IN CAPRICORN

The moon in Capricorn has an emotional seriousness, a sober orientation, and a practical awareness that brings with it a need to feel useful. Using the energies of the new moon and amplified ambitions of Capricorn, this is an ideal time to start new projects.

DECEMBER 30TH: FIRST QUARTER IN ARIES

The moon in Aries is emotionally direct and impulsive, with strong, influential feelings. Time for a fresh start, learning new behaviors, establishing new habits. Just don't rush to make decisions, as Aries is apt to do, feeling as though quicker is better. It's not. Take your time to consider what you need, what you want, and choose carefully. The choices made in Aries set the tone for the extended future.

RITUAL PLANNER

GOAL/INTENTION:

ITEMS NEEDED:

STEPS:

FINDING LIGHT WITHIN THE DARK

Despite December being the month when the sun is born anew, it can be a dark time for people. With long nights, short days, and cold weather, it's all too easy to slide into a winter-time funk. But, with a little magic, we can keep our lives full of light all through the dark half of the year. I'm prone to developing SAD, or Seasonal Affective Disorder, so my grimoire is full of charms, spells, and tips to keep the blues at bay. I picked my top three favorites to share with you.

Creative Inspiration Jar

This a good old-fashion witch jar to ensure that your creative flow isn't slowed down by the gloom of winter.
Suggested ingredients: glass jar with cork stopper, glitter, orange and yellow confetti, amethyst and/or amber beads; ground cinnamon; dragons blood resin; mint leaves or peppermint oil; cloves; dried lavender; something to represent or symbolize your artistic medium (i.e. bracelet charm that looks like a paintbrush, a photo of a computer or typewriter); acrylic paint or a paint pen to draw symbol or sigil for inspiration on the side of the jar; orange candle to seal the spell.

Lemon Life Charm (Get it? Lovin' life- Lemon Life- I know, Mom joke)

All you need for this Lemon Life charm is an oil diffuser bracelet and lemon (or your preferred citrus fruint) scented essential oil. Lemons are like the sun, bright and cheerful, and their scent is is refreshing, uplifting, and rejuvenating. Just add a few drops to the diffuser while you visualize the sun, bright and warm on your skin. The joyful scent of lemons will brighten your day whenever you catch their scent.

Mirror, Mirror, On the Wall

This simple decorating trick that will add light to a room even on the gloomiest of days. Placing a mirror on the wall opposite or next to a window will harness and reflect the light coming in. Give the light a magical boost by choosing your mirror based on the shape. According to GemsInStyle.com, the triangle represents the creative spirit as its' the dynamic force of creation; the square generates energy of stability, and the circle represents unity and the source of all creation. Another option would be to use color magic, choosing a mirror based on the color of the frame- i.e. a yellow or gold frame to give the room a cheerful, joyous feel.

DECEMBER FESTIVALS

The Iranian festival of Yalda, a celebration of the victory of light and goodness over darkness and evil, takes place on or around December 21st, or the Winter Solstice. According to Persian mythology, the god Mithra, who was born to a virgin mother on the Winter Solstice, symbolizes light, truth, goodness, strength, and friendship. Shab Chera, "night gazing", is honored by modern Persians who observe the holiday by staying up all night. The traditional food of this holiday consists of fruit and nuts, especially pomegranate and watermelon. The red color of these fruits symbolize Mithra and to invoke the crimson hues of dawn. [Source: https://en.wikipedia.org/wiki/List_of_multinational_festivals_and_holidays#December]

USE THE SPACE BELOW TO RECORD YOUR DECEMBER CELEBRATIONS

DECEMBER HERBS

Herbs of Prosperity

Winter is a time of stagnation, darkness, and cold, and so it goes to follow that money can become an issue. December comes with a lot of added expenses, with snow tires, high gas prices, holidays, taking personal days because of weather, heating expenses – the list goes on. But with a simple indoor herb garden containing the above herbs, you will have all you need to ensure your family doesn't struggle this winter. Make sachets, burn as incense, add to cooking, or tuck into decorative wreaths – however you wish to use them, they are sure to protect your family, ease your worries, and keep the cash flowing in.

HERB	SIZE/ SPREAD	START SEEDS INSIDE/OUTSIDE	HARDINESS ZONE	NATIVE REGION	GROWTH TYPE**	SUN SOIL
Basil	12-24"/ 12"	6-8/ anytime after	10-11	Central Africa, Southeast Asia	A	FS/F
Bay Laurel	10-60'/ 5-20	NR	8-10	Mediterranean	TP	FS/ V
Mint	12-24"/ 18"	NR	4-9	Mediterranean, Asia	P	PS/F
Rosemary	4-5'/ 4'	8-10/After	7-10	Mediterranean	TP	FS/V

*Weeks before or afer last spring frost

** A=Annual P=Perennial

** FS= full sun, PS= partial sun; WD= well-drained, M= moist, RM, rich moint, L= loamy, LS=loamy/sandy

Magic Properties:
Basil: Money, Wealth, Love, Relationships, Protection
Bay Laurel: Granting Wishes, Manifestation, Prosperity, Protection
Mint: Luck, Money, Healing, Love
Rosemary: Substitute for any herb, Ease Anxiety, Protection, Prosperity, Love, Luck

PAUSE & REFLECT

Go to your first prompt in this planner. You predicted the year, were you correct?

GRATITUDE LIST

MONTHLY TO-DO'S

TRY SOMETHING NEW

CRYSTALS

To make the most of your crystals' powers and energies, try making a crystal grid! A crystal grid is when you use at least four crystals and arrange them in the patterns of sacred geometry. Choose crystals with properties appropriate for your intention, then choose a shape that aligns with your goals. Draw the shape on a piece of paper, or, for a more permanent grid, use a pyrography pen to burn the shape into a plank of wood. If you wish to use a ready-made crystal grid, several volumes of the Book of Shadows special editions published by Witch Way Magazine every year. Cleanse and charge the crystals, put them on the grid, then take a moment to admire the grid. Then, with your intentions in the forefront of your mind, touch each stone, tracing the connecting lines between each stone. Using crystal grids boosts your power, and helps the magic manifest quicker and more efficiently.

Source: https://www.learnreligions.com/how-to-make-a-crystal-grid-4171722

CARD SPREAD

Card 1: What to give others - Card 2: What to give yourself - Card 3: What to give the world

SPELL

Productivity sachet: We all have those days – you know the kind I mean, when you wake up late and just can't seem to get anything done? Well, it was on one of these days that I came up with my Bee Productive sachet. With a square of cotton with a bumble bee pattern, 3 crystals (citrine, carnelian, and moss agate), and a bit of Success oil from the Witch Way magazine online shop, I put together a quick, easy, and surprisingly efficient productivity sachet. I took the stones in my hand and charged them by chanting: "I'm motivated, I'm moving, I'm doing what I need to! Each item on the list will get checked as done, simply by keeping these gems on my person." You can use this chant or make one up to better suit your needs. Then I anointed the stones with Witch Way Magazine's Success oil, wrapped them in the bumble bee cloth, and stuck it in my pocket. I was at my desk an hour later, getting my work done- and doing it well.

ENTITY

Visit a local cemetery with offerings such as flowers and stones. Visit graves that seem unvisited and leave them one of your offerings. .

SELF-CARE

Quiet time. Pick a few hours. That's your quiet time. Everyone must respect it.

TEA

Peppermint Tea - Black tea paired with peppermint leaves is a simple tea to combat the chaos of the holiday season. Sit, sip, and breathe.

HERBS

A tincture is an alcoholic extract of herbal constituents, according to Witchipedia.com. Tinctures are usually very potent, so only a few drops are used at a time. To make a tincture, fill a wide-mouthed jar with the herb(s) of choice, then add the alcohol. Put it in a dark, dry cabinet for a month or two, going in every few weeks to give it a shake. After the time is up, strain and jar.

28 NOVEMBER
MONDAY

29 NOVEMBER
TUESDAY

2 DECEMBER
FRIDAY

3 DECEMBER
SATURDAY

30 NOVEMBER
WEDNESDAY

1 DECEMBER
THURSDAY

4 DECEMBER
SUNDAY

DECEMBER - 2022

	M	T	W	T	F	S	S
48	28	29	30	1	2	3	4
49	5	6	7	8	9	10	11
50	12	13	14	15	16	17	18
51	19	20	21	22	23	24	25
52	26	27	28	29	30	31	1

5 DECEMBER
MONDAY

6 DECEMBER
TUESDAY

9 DECEMBER
FRIDAY

10 DECEMBER
SATURDAY

7 DECEMBER
WEDNESDAY

8 DECEMBER
THURSDAY

11 DECEMBER
SUNDAY

DECEMBER - 2022

	M	T	W	T	F	S	S
48	28	29	30	1	2	3	4
49	5	6	7	8	9	10	11
50	12	13	14	15	16	17	18
51	19	20	21	22	23	24	25
52	26	27	28	29	30	31	1

12 DECEMBER
MONDAY

13 DECEMBER
TUESDAY

16 DECEMBER
FRIDAY

17 DECEMBER
SATURDAY

14 DECEMBER
WEDNESDAY

15 DECEMBER
THURSDAY

18 DECEMBER
SUNDAY

DECEMBER - 2022

	M	T	W	T	F	S	S
48	28	29	30	1	2	3	4
49	5	6	7	8	9	10	11
50	12	13	14	15	16	17	18
51	19	20	21	22	23	24	25
52	26	27	28	29	30	31	1

19 DECEMBER
MONDAY

20 DECEMBER
TUESDAY

23 DECEMBER
FRIDAY

24 DECEMBER
SATURDAY

21 DECEMBER
WEDNESDAY

22 DECEMBER
THURSDAY

25 DECEMBER
SUNDAY

DECEMBER - 2022

	M	T	W	T	F	S	S
48	28	29	30	1	2	3	4
49	5	6	7	8	9	10	11
50	12	13	14	15	16	17	18
51	19	20	21	22	23	24	25
52	26	27	28	29	30	31	1

26 DECEMBER MONDAY

27 DECEMBER TUESDAY

30 DECEMBER FRIDAY

31 DECEMBER SATURDAY

28 DECEMBER
WEDNESDAY

29 DECEMBER
THURSDAY

1 JANUARY
SUNDAY

DECEMBER - 2022

	M	T	W	T	F	S	S
48	28	29	30	1	2	3	4
49	5	6	7	8	9	10	11
50	12	13	14	15	16	17	18
51	19	20	21	22	23	24	25
52	26	27	28	29	30	31	1

AUTHORS

TONYA A. BROWN

TONYA A. BROWN is a current resident of New Orleans, Louisiana, where she is the editor in chief of *Witch Way Magazine* as well as writer and host of the podcast *The Witch Daily Show.* Tonya is a Lenormand reader, medium, and magical guide for other witches. She has spoken at various events including Parliament of the World's Religions, and has written and edited various books on the occult.

*

Instagram @WitchWayMagazine

AMANDA WILSON

AMANDA WILSON, artist, witch, & SAHM strives to maintain balance between motherhood, witchcraft, and her blossoming career. Amanda's career is an amalgamation of duties: Columnist and Submissions Manager for *Witch Way Magazine*; executive assistant for The *Witch Daily Show* podcast; and content creator, contributing to Medium.com, Vocal.Media, and Hubpages.com. (It's no wonder she is passionate about planners!) To access online profiles or view her writing works, visit Amanda's author's website, www.WriteKindofMagic.art.

REFERENCES

"Composting At Home." *EPA*, Environmental Protection Agency, 10 Feb. 2021, www.epa.gov/recycle/composting-home.

Duffy, Jill. "How to Take Better Breaks to Boost Your Productivity." *PC-MAG*, PCMag, 30 Nov. 2020, www.pcmag.com/how-to/get-organized-how-to-take-better-breaks-to-boost-your-productivity.

Eilthireach. "Deeper into Lughnasadh." *Order of Bards, Ovates & Druids*, 15 Dec. 2019, druidry.org/druid-way/teaching-and-practice/druid-festivals/lughnasadh.

"Festival of Colours." *Holi*, Society for the Confluence of Festivals in India , 2021, www.holifestival.org/festival-of-colours.html.

"Festival of San Fermín." *Wikipedia*, Wikimedia Foundation, 12 Jan. 2021, en.wikipedia.org/wiki/Festival_of_San_Ferm%C3%ADn.

"Fête Du Vodoun." *Wikipedia*, Wikimedia Foundation, 23 Dec. 2020, en.wikipedia.org/wiki/F%C3%AAte_du_Vodoun.

Hughes, Kristoffer. *From the Cauldron Born: Exploring the Magic of Welsh Legend & Lore*. Kindle ed., Llewellyn Publications, 2012.

"In the Beginning". "The Early History of Bungee Jumping." *Mental Floss*, 13 July 2008, www.mentalfloss.com/article/19055/early-history-bungee-jumping.

"June Is LGBT Pride Month." *Youth.gov*, 2021, youth.gov/feature-article/june-lgbt-pride-month.

Luna, and Sol. "Crazy Facts About Life." *LonerWolf*, 13 Jan. 2021, lonerwolf.com/.

Metcalfe, Tom. "Operation Cone of Power: When British Witches Attacked Adolf Hitler." *Mental Floss*, 18 Oct. 2016, www.mentalfloss.com/article/86145/operation-cone-power-when-british-witches-attacked-adolf-hitler.

Moodymoons. "Weird Facts About Witchcraft & the Occult." *Moody Moons*, 2 Apr. 2018, www.moodymoons.com/2018/04/02/10-weird-facts-about-witchcraft-the-occult/.

"Moon Phases Calendar - January 2022, Lunar Calendar 2022 January." *Moon Calendar Astro-Seek*, mooncalendar.astro-seek.com/moon-phases-calendar-january-2022.

"The Moon's Transits through the Signs ." *Cafe Astrology .Com*, 2021, cafeastrology.com/whenthemoonisin.html.

Old Farmer's Almanac. "Gardening by the Moon." *Old Farmer's Almanac*, www.almanac.com/content/planting-by-the-moon.

"Parrtjima Festival." *Tourism Australia*, www.australia.com/en-us/events/arts-culture-and-music/parrtjima-festival.html.

Patterson, Rachel. *Kitchen Witchcraft: Garden Magic*. Moon Books, 2018.

Petersik, John, et al. "How To Make A $10 DIY Compost Bin." *Young House Love*, 2 Aug. 2018, www.younghouselove.com/younghouselovedotcompost/.

"TAPATI FESTIVAL." *EASTER ISLAND SPIRIT*, 18 Feb. 2021, www.easterislandspirit.com/tapati-festival/.

Tran, Sammy. "25 Arcane Facts About Spiritualism and the Occult in History." *Factinate*, 17 Aug. 2020, www.factinate.com/things/25-arcane-facts-spiritualism-occult-history/.

"Tuesday Is the Most Productive Day of the Week." *UCONN Health*, UCONN Health | Occupational and Environmental Medicine, 25 Dec. 2015, health.uconn.edu/occupational-environmental/wp-content/uploads/sites/25/2015/12/tuesday_most_productive.pdf.

Vanderlinden, Colleen. "How to Make a Compost Bin Using a Plastic Storage Container." *The Spruce*, www.thespruce.com/compost-bin-from-plastic-storage-container-2539493.

Walton, Alice G. "7 Ways Meditation Can Actually Change The Brain." *Forbes*, Forbes Magazine, 17 Jan. 2018, www.forbes.com/sites/alicegwalton/2015/02/09/7-ways-meditation-can-actually-change-the-brain/?sh=2e201d7b1465.

"Wand." *Wikipedia*, Wikimedia Foundation, 16 Feb. 2021, en.wikipedia.org/wiki/Wand.

WITCH WAY
PUBLISHING

CPSIA information can be obtained
at www.ICGtesting.com
Printed in the USA
BVHW061206190122
626621BV00003B/159